Benefits Realization from Information Technology

Benefits Realization from Information Technology

Colin Ashurst
Senior Teaching Fellow, Durham Business School, UK

First published 2012 by
PALGRAVE MACMILLAN

Palgrave Macmillan in the UK is an imprint of Macmillan Publishers Limited, registered in England, company number 785998, of Houndmills, Basingstoke, Hampshire RG21 6XS.

Palgrave Macmillan in the US is a division of St Martin's Press LLC, 175 Fifth Avenue, New York, NY 10010.

Palgrave Macmillan is the global academic imprint of the above companies and has companies and representatives throughout the world.

Palgrave® and Macmillan® are registered trademarks in the United States, the United Kingdom, Europe and other countries.

ISBN: 978–0–230–28959–8

This book is printed on paper suitable for recycling and made from fully managed and sustained forest sources. Logging, pulping and manufacturing processes are expected to conform to the environmental regulations of the country of origin.

A catalogue record for this book is available from the British Library.

A catalog record for this book is available from the Library of Congress.

10 9 8 7 6 5 4 3 2 1
21 20 19 18 17 16 15 14 13 12

Printed and bound in the United States of America

Contents

List of Tables   viii

List of Figures   ix

List of Boxes   x

Preface and Acknowledgements   xi

1 **Introduction**   1
   The paradox of IT: opportunities and failures   1
   Key themes in outline   2
   The structure of the rest of the book   3

2 **Foundations**   6
   Equipping the organization: developing the
     benefits realization capability   6
   A benefits-driven approach to investments in IT   8
   From a benefits-led approach to a benefits
     realization capability   9

3 **Benefits Realization Capability**   10
   The big picture   10
   Capabilities, competences and practices   11
   Framework for the benefits realization capability   15
   The framework provides a foundation for the research   19

4 **Insights into Current Adoption of
   Benefits-Driven Approaches**   20
   The research   20
   Findings related to each competence   21
   Discussion: key themes emerging from the
     analysis of the case studies   28
   Implications for practice   30

5 **Succeeding with Benefits Realization**   32
   The research   32
   Introduction to the case-study organization   32
   Lessons learned: developing competences for
     successful business transformation   34

Succeeding with business transformation 43
Looking ahead 45

6 **The Challenges of Benefits Realization** 46
The research 46
Findings from the research 47
Discussion: key themes emerging from the research 55
Looking ahead 58

7 **Benefits Realization from the IT Portfolio** 60
Portfolio perspective: a critical element of
the benefits realization capability 60
A framework for the IT portfolio 62
Practices for benefits realization from
IT portfolio management 65
Benefits planning 66
Benefits delivery 71
Benefits exploitation 76
Benefits review 77
Overall picture – a lack of focus on the IT portfolio 80

8 **Building the Capability – Breaking out
of the Catch-22** 82
Building an organizational capability for
benefits realization 82
Realizing benefits from IT 83
The development of benefits realization competences 85
Building the benefits realization capability 87
Succeeding in breaking out of the
techno-centric mindset 90

9 **Big Picture** 93
Context – competitive advantage from IT 93
Project perspective 94
Portfolio perspective 99
Organizational perspective 105
Summary 108

10 **Practices and the Development of Competences
for Benefits Realization** 109
Practices in practice 109
Principles for benefits realization: a new mindset
and the basis for a 'common language' 112

Patterns as a way of capturing and sharing practices:
knowledge management and organizational learning   114
Common project framework   118
Develop craft skills to enable benefits realization   119
Building competences through organizational learning   119

11 **Making a Difference – First Steps in a Change Programme**   **120**
Introduction   120
Findings from engagement with IT projects   125
Learning about IT projects and ways of working   130
Developing the benefits realization capability of
the organization   131
Learning about the approach to the research   133
Conclusions   135
Conundrum   136

12 **Reflections on Research Methods**   **137**
Context   137
Aim of the research   138
Philosophy and strategy: the foundations for
the research programme   139
Case studies   147
Action research   149
Adopting an agile approach to research projects   153
Implications for further work   157

13 **Looking Ahead – Implications and Opportunities**   **158**
Progress so far   158
Practical implications   160
Policy and wider implications   162
Looking ahead   164

Appendices   **178**
*Appendix 1: outline of the research programme
and related deliverables*   178
Appendix 2: a framework of practices for benefits realization   182
*Appendix 3: Summary of findings from
empirical work (Chapter 6)*   187
*Appendix 4: outline of maturity levels for
key factors (Chapter 6)*   189

References   191

Index   199

Tables

3.1	Definitions of key competences for benefits realization	17
3.2	Practices for benefits planning	18
5.1	The three projects examined in the case study	34
5.2	Examples of practices adopted to enable effective team working	38
7.1	Practices for an exploratory project	71
8.1	Barriers to the development of a benefits realization capability	87
8.2	Important elements of a change programme to develop the benefits realization capability	92
11.1	Initial view of challenges affecting benefits realization	122
11.2	Projects within the overall programme	123
13.1	Implications of dynamic capabilities for benefits realization: findings from empirical work	173

Figures

3.1	Benefits realization competences	16
6.1	Competences – within the 'black box' of the formal organization	57
7.1	The IT and change portfolio building on Ward and Peppard (2002) and McFarlan (1981)	63
7.2	A portfolio-level perspective of IT systems within an organization	64
10.1	Exploring risk management as a practice at different levels of granularity	110

Boxes

3.1	The value of practices	14
5.1	The role of the sponsor of a major project	37
5.2	Factors contributing to the success of transformation projects at the council	42
5.3	Factors contributing to the development of the transformation capability at the council	45
6.1	Drivers for change	48
7.1	Summary of practices for IT portfolio management by competence	65
7.2	A broader perspective on IT investment appraisal	68
7.3	An example of issues in application lifecycle management	75
7.4	Examples of practices for benefits exploitation	76
9.1	The toolkit of practices for benefits realization	94
9.2	Project-level starting points for developing benefits realization competences	99
9.3	Approaches to sharing learning	107
10.1	Succeeding with investments in IT – principles for a benefits-driven approach	113
10.2	A simple example of the patterns format for capturing and sharing knowledge	117
13.1	Key questions for further research	170

Preface and Acknowledgements

Benefits realization from Information Technology (IT) is a critical business and policy issue. The continued failure of high-profile, public sector IT projects is only one example of the challenges. Checkland, Clegg, Eason, Markus, Ward and others have carried out excellent research in this area over many years but there has been limited impact on practice. I take this earlier work as a starting point (Benefits Management, Technochange, socio-technical approaches, etc.) and explore the challenges of putting the ideas into practice to enable organizations to succeed in benefits realization from IT.

My early research consisted of case studies, which established a working model for the benefits realization capability of the organization and uses the idea of 'practices' (cf. routines) to focus on what individuals and groups actually do (Ashurst et al., 2008). The ongoing research is now primarily participative action research tackling the challenge of enabling organizations and individuals to realize benefits from IT.

The book provides a fresh perspective on the challenges of benefits realization from IT. It draws on recent and ongoing research to explore how to build the organizational capability to realize the strategic potential of IT. It tackles the chasm between theory and practice and explores how to gain wider adoption of successful socio-technical and benefits-driven approaches to investments in IT.

The book is aimed at academics, working in the Information Systems area, including PhD students, policy makers and influencers, and business and IT managers interested in this area, or taking a postgraduate qualification with strategic IT content. I hope that pulling together the findings from the ongoing stream of research in one place will provide readers with useful insights.

I am deeply indebted to many for their advice and support. I would particularly like to thank Peter Murray and John Ward. The long association with them at Cranfield was critical in this research and in starting my second career as a teacher and researcher. I also value the continuing support and advice of Neil Doherty and Joe Peppard as PhD supervisors and colleagues in this work. Their input was also essential. Dr Julie Hodges was a collaborator in the work that under-pins Chapter 6; she provided valuable insights. Business colleagues, for example, through the North East IT Directors Forum, students and many others have also made huge contributions. The flaws of course are my own. Your thoughts and comments will be valued.

1
Introduction

In this chapter I set out the motivation for the work in terms of the opportunities provided by IT and the continuing failure rate of IT projects. The chapter concludes with a brief introduction to the key themes of the book.

The paradox of IT: opportunities and failures

Innovation in IT is continuing at a rapid pace and will continue to provide new opportunities for organizations. IT has a critical role to play in the success of all sizes of organization, from the one-person start-up to the very largest:

> *I really think that the way companies implement business processes, organizational change, and IT-driven innovation is what differentiates the leaders from the laggers. Rather than leveling the playing field, IT is actually leading to greater discrepancies. In most industries the top companies are pulling further away from the companies in the middle and the bottom of the competitive spectrum.* (Erik Brynjolfsson, *MIT Sloan Management Review*, Spring 2010)

One of the factors that sets apart the leaders is their ability to realize benefits from IT-enabled change.

The primary driver for my research which provides a foundation for this book, was the continuing failure of organizations to realize the full potential of investments in IT. This is seen in the continuing high failure rates of investments in IT in terms of benefits delivered, which have stayed at around 70–80 per cent over the past 30 years (Eason, 1988; Clegg, 1997; BCS, 2004). Socio-technical approaches and benefits-driven approaches for IT have been available for over ten years (Avison et al., 1998; Mumford, 1995; Ward et al., 1996), but the lack of improvement in project-success rates suggests that they have had limited impact on how organizations approach IT investments in practice.

The research programme that underpins this book is seeking to gain insights into how organizations can develop the competences required to succeed in realizing the potential of investments in IT to deliver benefits to stakeholders and improve organizational performance. Appendix 1 provides an outline of the research projects that form the background to this book.

Key themes in outline

A 'fourth era' of IT is proposed (Ward and Peppard, 2002) based on the concept of an IS capability being the enabler of competitive advantage from IT; that is, sustained competitive advantage comes not from any one project or solution but from the ability continually to deliver solutions that provide a stream of temporary sources of advantage. Empirical studies (e.g. Santhanam and Hartono, 2003) have indicated a strong link between IT capability and firm performance, and suggest that there is an opportunity to get a sustained advantage.

The idea of an IS capability or 'benefits realization capability' is particularly relevant to the challenge of benefits realization from investments in IT, as it facilitates exploration of the organization as a whole and not just the IT function. In the book I provide a framework for this benefits realization capability and use the idea of 'practices' to contribute to the development of the capability in organizations.

A number of key themes are developed through the book as follows.

Benefits from IT come from people doing things differently, not from the technology itself; that is, benefits arise from how people *use* the technology and information. This means that realizing benefits from IT is an organization-wide issue, which requires leadership from all areas and levels of the organization. Previous work (e.g.

Benefits Management – Ward and Daniel, 2006) provides guidance on benefits-led approaches to IT investments.

IT investments are increasingly contributing to business innovation, resulting in new products, services and ways of working. In many cases projects require multidisciplinary teamwork. Benefits-led approaches must support these teams, enabling them to work together effectively in a wide range of situations. In many cases there will be a drive to innovate to create new sources of value rather than simply solving clear-cut problems to improve efficiency or effectiveness.

Successful completion of a benefits-led investment in IT is only the start of benefits realization. There must be a focus on benefits exploitation through the life of an IT system. This area has been neglected.

Benefits realization requires a focus on portfolio management and organizational perspectives as well as the management of individual projects. For example, 'which projects should we invest in?' is a key question, which has to be considered at a portfolio level.

There is a considerable gap between what we know about the value of benefits-led approaches and the extent of effective adoption of these approaches in organizations. A key challenge is overcoming this 'knowing–doing' gap. I tackle this from the perspective of developing an organizational capability for benefits realization. Developing the benefits realization capability is a strategic change programme, which involves changing attitudes and behaviour – not just the adoption of a new approach to projects.

The structure of the rest of the book

Chapter 2: Foundations

A brief introduction to previous work in the areas of benefits realization and IT capabilities establishes foundations for the rest of the book.

Chapter 3: Benefits Realization Capability

A framework of competences and practices for benefits realization.

Chapter 4: Insights into Current Adoption of Benefits-Driven Approaches

The chapter draws on 45 case studies to provide insights into the current adoption of benefits-driven approaches and to provide evidence of the value of the practices/competence approach.

Chapter 5: Succeeding with Benefits Realization

Results from an in-depth case study of an organization succeeding with benefits realization and developing the organizational benefits realization capability.

Chapter 6: The Challenges of Benefits Realization

Insights from a wide-ranging exploratory study to understand how business and IT managers perceived the challenges they faced in building the benefits realization capability of the organization. The chapter provides important context for exploring the action required to develop this benefits realization capability.

Chapter 7: Benefits Realization from the IT Portfolio

Many aspects of benefits realization relate to the IT portfolio rather than individual IT projects (e.g. which projects to invest in). The chapter provides a portfolio perspective on benefits realization competences and practices.

Chapter 8: Building the Capability – Breaking Out of the Catch-22

The chapter draws on several empirical projects to explore the barriers to the adoption of benefits-driven approaches, and how they can be overcome. It makes the case that developing a benefits realization capability within an organization is itself a benefits-driven change programme. So organizations are stuck in a catch-22: to succeed in developing the benefits realization capability, they already need the capability in place. The chapter sets out some ways forward.

Chapter 9: Big Picture

The chapter sets out our current view of the framework as it has evolved to date.

Chapter 10: Practices and the Development of Competences for Benefits Realization

The chapter includes a deeper look at how 'practices' contribute to organizational competences, drawing on the idea of patterns and making connections with ideas of knowledge management and organizational learning. It provides further insights into how organizations can approach the development of competences for benefits realization.

Chapter 11: Making a Difference – First Steps in a Change Programme

The chapter draws on an ongoing action research programme which is seeking to develop the benefits realization capability of a large organization (a Russell Group University). The chapter outlines the approach and the initial results to provide some starting points for other organizations.

Chapter 12: Reflections on Research Methods

I will keep the discussion of research methods very brief in earlier chapters and use this opportunity to reflect on the research approach and how it has evolved. The aim is to share lessons learned for others adopting a participative approach to case studies and action research. I draw in part on a recent conference paper where I explored the possibility of a more 'agile' approach to research.

Chapter 13: Looking Ahead – Implications and Opportunities

In the final chapter, I will set out the implications of the work for policy and practice *and will set out future research directions.*

2
Foundations

A brief introduction to previous work in the areas of benefits realization and IT capabilities to establish foundations for the rest of the book.

Equipping the organization: developing the benefits realization capability

Melville et al. (2004) developed a model that shows key factors involved in linking IT resources with organizational performance. The model makes it clear that technology by itself is not the direct source of value, but that complementary organizational resources are required and that the value is realized through business processes. Markus (2004) also emphasizes the importance of organizational change, not just technology delivery, to realize benefits.

The concept of an 'IS capability' as the source of organizational advantage from IT is a second starting point for this research. This was highlighted as an important area for further research by Peppard and Ward (2004: p. 189): 'research to examine and understand how IS competencies and capability can be developed and sustained will provide a source of real value to organizations'. Ward and Peppard (2002) suggest that we are moving into a 'fourth era' of IT based on the concept of an IS capability being the enabler of competitive advantage from IT. That is, sustained competitive advantage does not come from any one project or solution, but it comes from the ability continually to deliver solutions that provide a stream of temporary sources of advantage.

Other works also emphasize the importance of this perspective (Wade and Hulland, 2004; Santhanam and Hartono, 2003). The competences related to realizing value from IT relate to changing the organization and are 'dynamic capabilities' (Teece et al., 1997). The similarity Eisenhardt and Martin (2000) identify across organizations in the underlying 'routines' that enable gradual, incremental development of these dynamic capabilities is highly relevant to this research.

Work from many different perspectives, for example by Doherty et al. (2003), Eason (1988), Ward et al. (1996), Avison et al. (1998), Mumford (1995) and Farbey et al. (1999), identifies major shortcomings in the approaches taken in practice to IT projects. In addition, the focus of many efforts to improve IT project-success rates has been on improving the project process with well-defined methodologies and even comprehensive software tools. Given the evidence from Nandhakumar and Avison (1999) that traditional methodologies are treated primarily as a *necessary fiction* to present an image of control, further efforts to drive improvement to project-success rates simply by improving 'methodologies' seem unlikely to succeed.

The focus of this programme of research on organizational competences provides an opportunity to take a different perspective; more related to how people actually work, than a focus on a 'project methodology'. The challenge is how to operationalize the broad concept of an IS competence and provide guidance for managers and project teams. As an example, Peppard and Ward (2004) define 26 competences, but these are not defined other than in a very brief description. Work is taking place (e.g. Caldeira et al., 2006) to refine an overall model of competences, but existing research has not addressed *how* these competences can be developed.

Practice is an increasingly widely used term, within the organizational literature, and a range of descriptions and definitions have emerged. Wenger et al. (2002: p. 38) suggest the following definition: 'a set of socially defined ways of doing things in a specific domain: a set of common approaches and shared standards that create a basis for action, problem solving, performance and accountability.' Not only does the concept of a practice appear to be closely aligned with how people actually work (Brown and Duguid, 2000), but it is also particularly relevant in knowledge-intensive activities, such as IS projects (Waterson et al., 1997) where much of the effort is based upon the experiences of individuals and teams. Moreover, the concept of practice relates to the informal organization and how work is *actually* done by individuals and groups. It fits well with the approach to 'methodology' as a framework and guidelines rather than prescriptive rules (Iivari and Huisman, 2007). Improvements in benefits realization will come from putting ideas into practice and approaches that enable the multidisciplinary teams involved in these projects to work together effectively.

The use of competence and practice perspectives for this research is based on strong foundations in wider management literature and was intended as a basis for exploring the practicalities of projects and programmes of business transformation.

A benefits-driven approach to investments in IT

Conceptually, a benefits-driven approach to investments in IT is straightforward. It is built on the principles that IT has no inherent value and that the benefits come from using IT to enable *people* to do things differently (Peppard et al., 2007). Therefore, the starting point of a project is to consider relevant stakeholders and what they are going to do differently because of the investment and how this is of benefit to them. This focus on benefits for the customer/stakeholder is increasingly valuable as IT is now at the core of the delivery of products and services and is no longer just about automation of internal processes and the replacement of people with technology.

From this starting point, a project then focuses on identifying and delivering the organizational changes required to achieve the potential benefits; these changes are supported and enabled by IT. Benefits come from approaching these investments as 'technochange' – projects that combine technology delivery and organizational change to deliver value for the customers and other stakeholders.

One potentially important mechanism for proactively managing the social and organizational impacts of an IT project is 'Benefits Management', which can be defined as *'the process of organizing and managing, such that the potential benefits arising from the use of IT are actually realized'* (Ward and Daniel, 2006: p. 36; my emphasis). Benefits Management builds on a core set of principles and provides a process and a set of management practices for planning and leading a benefits-driven project. As benefits come from organizational change – from enabling people to do things differently, a key implication is that there is a need for business ownership of benefits and the changes required to realize them. Benefits Management provides a coherent framework and common language for business staff, managers and IT professionals to work together effectively to make change happen and to realize the benefits.

From a benefits perspective, improving the success rate of investments in IT is not just an issue for the IT function. New project methodologies, new software development tools, outsourcing and offshoring can only ever be a part of a solution. Improvements must address the competences of the organization as a whole.

From a benefits-led approach to a benefits realization capability

Benefits-led approaches are effective in practice but are not widely adopted. We have reframed the challenges of gaining adoption of a benefits-led approach to investments in IT as the development of an organizational benefits realization capability. In the rest of this book, we explore how organizations can develop this capability.

3
Benefits Realization Capability

A framework of competences and practices for benefits realization is described following a brief introduction to the resource-based perspective of an organization and the general concepts of competences and capabilities.

The big picture

The primary issue we are tackling is enabling organizations to succeed in realizing benefits from investments in IT. These benefits may be for customers, employees, other stakeholders of the organization, for the organization itself and its shareholders. We are following the principles that:

1. IT has no inherent value.
2. Benefits arise when IT enables 'people to do things differently' (Ward and Daniel, 2006).

This is consistent with the idea of 'technochange' (Markus, 2004), which states that value is realized from investments in IT when the investment is managed as part of a project or programme of organizational change. Value is realized when the focus is on delivering benefits for stakeholders rather than just on delivery of an IT solution. The shift to a focus on benefits affects the business case and the overall life cycle of the investment.

Benefits realization from IT investments can be conceptualized as an organizational capability that has the purpose of ensuring that investments made in IT consistently generate value. The capability consists of a number of distinct, yet complementary, competences.

Capabilities, competences and practices

Resources, capabilities, competences and practices are all important concepts that have already received much attention in the general and strategic management literatures (e.g. Barney, 1991; Grant, 1996b; Teece et al., 1997; Brown and Duguid, 2000; Helfat and Peteraf, 2003). In this section, we illustrate how these theoretical constructs can be applied to the task of delivering specified benefits from IT investments.

Over the past twenty-five years, there has been a significant interest in how organizations can assemble a unique portfolio of resources that will render them a competitive advantage. The resource-based view (RBV) of the firm (Wernerfelt, 1984; Barney, 1991) suggests that organizations should invest in those assets and resources that they believe will best assist them in successfully gaining a sustainable competitive advantage. In this context, resources have been defined as 'stocks of available factors that are owned or controlled by the firm' (Amit and Schoemaker, 1993). However, from a competitive perspective not all resources are equally valuable. An organization's primary source of competitive advantage will be through those resources that are simultaneously valuable, rare, imperfectly imitable and non-substitutable – the so-called VRIN conditions (Barney, 1991). Whilst resources are clearly a critical element of the RBV, there is a growing recognition that resources, *per se*, do not create value. Rather, value is created by an organization's ability to mobilize, marshal and utilize these resources, through the application of capabilities and competences (Black and Boal, 1994; Bowman and Ambrosini, 2000; Grant, 1996a). It can be argued that organizations will only attain a sustainable competitive advantage if they can assemble a set of competences that can be consistently applied (Teece and Pisano, 1994) and that competitors find difficult to imitate (Barney, 1991; Prahalad and Hamel, 1990).

This analysis can be applied to the realization of benefits from IT investments. All organizations should establish a benefits realization capability, whether IT is a source of competitive advantage or not. However, this capability cannot be developed within the boundaries of the IT function; research demonstrates the need for enterprise-wide cooperation and engagement to realize the benefits from IT investments (Ward and Peppard, 2004). In delivering value through IT, the key resource is not technology but knowledge and this knowledge will be distributed throughout the organization. As Newell et al. (2004) have noted, the primary challenge for project teams, set up to design and implement a large-scope IT system, is to coordinate and integrate such distributed knowledge.

There is a lack of precision in the usage of terms and concepts surrounding the RBV perspective, which needs to be addressed, particularly with respect to the distinction between a competence and a capability:

- **Competence** refers to a 'firm's capacity to deploy resources, usually in combination, using organizational processes, to effect a desired end' (Amit and Shoemaker, 1993: p. 35). A competence is thus an attribute of a team, function or even the entire organization. Each competence is underpinned by the skills, knowledge and experiences of employees, that is people resources, who are likely to be distributed enterprise-wide, and deployed in combination with specific organizational processes and resources (McGrath et al., 1995).
- **Capability** is a higher-level construct than a competence (Stalk et al., 1992), defined and enacted through the application of a set of competences (Teece et al., 1997; Kangas, 1999; Moingeon et al., 1998). More specifically, a capability can be defined as an organization's ability to 'perform a set of co-ordinated tasks, utilizing organizational resources, for the purposes of achieving a particular end result' (Helfat and Peteraf, 2003: p. 1000).

Benefits realization from IT investments can be considered as an organizational capability that has the express purpose of ensuring that investments made in IT consistently generate value, through the enactment of a number of distinct, yet complementary, competences. However, whilst it appears to make sense to conceptualize benefits realization as a capability underpinned by a number of distinct competences, such a model is still at a relatively high level of granularity. Competences have been referred to as an 'amorphous heap' (Wernerfelt, 1984) as little is generally known about the knowledge resources that underpin them, nor how this knowledge should be co-ordinated and integrated. Consequently, the practitioner will almost certainly be left asking questions as to how specific benefits realization competences might best be developed, and ultimately managed, whilst the researcher will want to know how they can observe and measure such high-level constructs, when conducting empirical research (Black and Boal, 1994; Miller and Shamsie, 1996).

One potentially rewarding way of adding granularity to a benefits realization competence is by decomposing it into a number of constituent practices, each of which is underpinned by the skills, knowledge and experiences of organizational employees and sometimes those employees of external entities. Carlile (2002) contends that practices are strongly focused upon their *objects* and *ends*, which make practices far more concrete and observable than competences. Not only does the concept of a practice appear to be closely aligned with how people *actually* work, it is also particularly relevant for IS projects, where much of the effort is based upon the knowledge and experiences of individuals and teams (Newell et al., 2004). Moreover, the concept of practice relates to the informal organization and how individuals and teams discharge their responsibilities. In contrast, management literature tends to emphasize processes and procedures, defined by the formal organization, which focus upon prescriptions of how the work should be done, and in so doing, often ignore many critical factors that affect performance (Brown and Duguid, 2000).

Based primarily on Wenger et al.'s (2002) definition, but also taking account of other appropriate sources (e.g. Brown and Duguid, 2000; Schultze and Boland, 2000; Grant, 1996b; and Carlile, 2002) I established the following working definition of *practice*, for the purpose of this study:

> *a set of socially defined ways of doing things, in a specific domain, to achieve a defined – and generally measurable – outcome, and create the basis for responding appropriately to individual circumstances.*

From this definition, a number of phrases require further clarification, as they have a significant impact upon the way in which it can be used to identify appropriate practices.

Socially defined ways of doing things: *Socially defined* implies that a practice is inherently people oriented: it relates to 'the activities of people' (Brown and Duguid, 2000; my emphasis). As Schultze and Boland (2000) note, the term practice is used deliberately to capture the essence of *what people actually do*, as underpinned by their knowledge, skills and experience, and evidenced through their behaviour.

In a specific domain: Given the study's explicit focus on benefits realization, we were only interested in those practices that might directly contribute to managing the realization of benefits from systems development projects.

To achieve a defined – and generally measurable – outcome: All practices should have a clear and specified benefits-oriented aim. As Carlile (2002) notes, practices are typically defined in terms of their 'means' and most importantly their 'ends', which allow the success of the practice to be demonstrated.

Creates the basis for responding appropriately to individual circumstances: A practice is not a set of highly formalized rules that prescribe in detail the way an activity should be undertaken. As Schultze and Boland (2000: p. 204) note, it is not *'a mechanical reaction to rules, norms or models, but a strategic, regulated improvisation responding to the situation'* (my emphasis).

Each benefits realization competence is underpinned by a closely related suite of benefits realization practices, which, in their totality help to define the competence. Box 3.1 highlights aspects of the value of practices.

Box 3.1 The value of practices

Practices are what people do. From our research, we are evolving a set of practices, which form a 'toolkit' for benefits realization. The toolkit approach enables flexibility: applying the right tools at the right time and adapted as necessary to the specific situation. The tools also provide a common language, which enables improvisation as multidisciplinary teams work together. The jazz metaphor is a helpful way of thinking about teamwork between the skilled professionals involved in benefits-driven IT projects.

The toolkit approach can also be applied to many of the human-centred practices, brainstorming for example, which are such an important part of effective working. We use the framework provided by work on *patterns* (see Chapter 10) as a way of capturing and sharing the rich knowledge involved in practice to build up a toolkit for benefits realization.

Appendix 2 contains the initial framework of practices (Ashurst et al., 2008). We have since evolved this into a 'toolkit' that provides a working outline of each practice as a basis for sharing knowledge and to underpin further action research.

There is a benefit from adopting individual practices in response to the needs of the organization. There is also value in adopting a range of practices as part of a broader programme of action to develop the capability of the organization to realize benefits from the portfolio of investments in IT.

4 competences

Framework for the benefits realization capability

The benefits realization capability comprises four distinct, yet highly interrelated, competences (see Figure 3.1 and Table 3.1).

Benefits planning: benefits do not simply emerge, as if by magic, from the introduction of a new technology; their realization needs to be carefully planned and managed. Benefits planning includes a strategic perspective, enabling innovation and deciding which projects to undertake, as well as benefits-focused planning of individual projects.

Benefits planning is defined as 'the ability to effectively identify the planned outcomes of an IS development project and make explicit the means by which they will be achieved' (Ashurst et al., 2008). As such, this process should operate at two distinct levels. First, the IS/IT strategy should present a broad overview of how the planned portfolio of IS applications will support the realization of business benefits and in so doing directly contribute to corporate objectives. Secondly, benefits planning should be conducted, in detail, for every individual project.

Benefits delivery: benefits primarily arise from the organizational change that accompanies an IT implementation, rather than directly from the technology itself. The benefits and related changes need to be the focus of activity.

Benefits delivery can be defined as 'the ability to design and execute the programme of organizational change necessary to realize all of the benefits specified in the benefits plan' (Ashurst et al., 2008). Consequently, benefits delivery typically relates to project initiation, after approval of the business case or benefits realization plan, through to completion of the project. Benefits delivery focuses upon the organizational changes necessary to achieve benefits, rather than the delivery of the technical solution. The organizational environment in which the project takes place is likely to have a significant impact on the attitudes and actions of the project team and wider stakeholders.

Benefits review: organizations must monitor and evaluate results on an ongoing basis. This will improve the results of individual projects and will ensure that the organization's ability to deliver business value improves over time.

Benefits review can be defined as 'the organization's ability to effectively assess the success of the project in terms of the benefits already delivered and the identification of the ways and means by which further benefits might be realized' (Ashurst et al., 2008). Benefits review is an *ongoing activity*: plans are reviewed and adjusted, delivered benefits are reviewed and modified, and the ongoing exploitation requires ongoing review. Benefits review is also conceived as being an ideal opportunity for organizational learning, so that the organization's capability to succeed in the realization of benefits can be enhanced over a period.

Benefits exploitation: the quest to leverage benefits from business software should not cease as soon as it has been implemented. Continued focus is required over the life of the investment.

Benefits exploitation can be defined as 'the adoption of the portfolio of practices required to realize the potential benefits from information, applications and IT services, over their operational life'

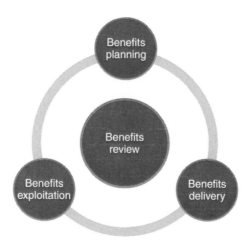

Figure 3.1   Benefits realization competences

Table 3.1 Definitions of key competences for benefits realization

Competence	Definition (Ashurst et al., 2008)
Benefits planning	'the ability to identify valuable opportunities for IT investments and to effectively identify the planned outcomes of an IT development project and make explicit the means by which they will be achieved'
Benefits delivery	'the ability to design and execute the programmes of organizational change necessary to realize all of the benefits specified in the benefits plan'
Benefits review	'the organization's ability to effectively assess the success of projects in terms of the benefits already delivered and the identification of the ways and means by which further benefits might be realized'
Benefits exploitation	'the adoption of the portfolio of practices required to realize the potential benefits from information, applications and IT services, over their operational life'

(Ashurst et al., 2008). This is important; in many scenarios there is a need for a process of ongoing learning and incremental improvement to realize further benefits that is not the subject of any further IS *project* activity.

Competences have both explicit and tacit elements and can be hard for managers to deal with. One way of adding granularity to a benefits realization competence is through adoption of a *toolkit* of *practices*, each of which can be tailored to the needs and circumstances of a specific organization.

Given the relative immaturity of the IT benefits-realization literature, it was necessary to conduct a broader review of the IS literature, to identify potentially relevant benefits realization practices. In particular, contributions from the socio-technical (e.g. Doherty and King, 2005; Clegg, 2000), IT-enabled-change (e.g. Markus, 2004; Markus and Benjamin, 1997; Hughes and Scott Morton, 2006) and IT-evaluation (e.g. Farbey et al., 1993; Remenyi and Sherwood-Smith, 1999) literatures were found to be very useful; they all have a strong focus on stakeholder involvement, project outcomes and organizational change. These literatures presented insights into the various approaches, techniques or behaviours that might help to facilitate benefits realization.

Examples from the initial set of practices are included in Table 3.2. See Appendix 2 for the full set of practices.

Table 3.2 Practices for benefits planning (examples)

Code	Practice	Description	Output	Literature
BP1	Identify strategic drivers	'Top-down' activity to clarify the strategic/business drivers for the project and its contribution to the achievement of business strategy.	Strategic drivers analysis	Ward and Elvin, 1999 Ward and Daniel, 2006
BP2	Analyse stakeholder expectations	Conduct a structured, 'bottom-up' analysis of the stakeholder's requirements, in terms of delivered benefits.	Analysis of expectations by stakeholder	Edwards and Peppard, 1997 Neely et al., 2002
BP3	Identify and define benefits	Review of strategic drivers and the stakeholder requirements, to identify/agree the target benefits.	Benefits analysis including agreed measures, targets and benefit owners	Peppard and Ward, 2005
BP4	Establish benefit/process interactions	Relate the benefits to business processes to identify where changes will take place and help identify relevant measures. Assess the variability and uncertainty in the process and consider the implications for benefits realization.	Process/benefit map	Ward and Peppard, 2002 Bohn, 1994 Brooke, 2000 Ward and Daniel, 2006 Bashein et al., 1994
BP5	Establish benefit/stakeholder interactions	Identify stakeholder groups affected by the technology, and changes required to realize the benefits. Identify business change issues and actions required including communication and engagement with the stakeholders, and the redesign of job specifications.	Stakeholder impact assessment	Eason, 1988 Joshi, 1991 Benjamin and Levinson, 1993 Doolin, 2004

The framework provides a foundation for the research

The framework of competences and practices was established at an early stage of the research programme. It provides a foundation for later stages of the work.

4
Insights into Current Adoption of Benefits-Driven Approaches

This chapter draws on 45 case studies to provide insights into the current adoption of benefits-driven approaches and to provide evidence of the value of the practices/competence approach. Thanks to Neil Doherty and Joe Peppard: an extended and revised version of this chapter is found in Ashurst et al. (2008).

The research

The research was designed as an exploratory study to provide new insights into benefits realization from IT investments. A case-study approach was adopted to ensure that the benefits realization capability could be explored from different organizational perspectives. The overall goal was to 'explore the extent to which organizations have adopted benefits-driven practices when undertaking investments in IT' and, as a result, to gain insight into the practices required to realize the benefits, and how to secure adoption of benefits-driven approaches.

More specifically, our aim was to review critically the conduct of information systems development projects, in a sample of case organizations, to explore the extent to which the approaches and methods they utilized mapped onto our framework of competences and practices. In so doing, we anticipated extending our initial framework through the identification of new practices, as well as exploring the extent to which existing practices were deployed.

Five cases were studied in two phases.

A sample of 25 case projects from an IT consultancy knowledge base was used to gain a broader perspective on the adoption of benefits-related approaches and to gain an initial insight into the value of the practices approach. These projects were the focus of a first phase of empirical work. These cases provide the main basis for the discussion that follows.

A sample of 20 consulting projects, undertaken by the author, that built on the sample from the knowledge base. They provided wider insights into the organizational factors that affect both the success of projects and the adoption of benefits-related approaches and helped in preparation for the in-depth cases studies that followed in a later research project.

Findings related to each competence

Findings related to each benefits realization competence are discussed in this section. The findings are linked to:

- Specific practices: for example, (BP2: identify strategic drivers). There is a full list of the practices in Appendix 2.
- Project and document that provide the evidence: for example, (Vision and Scope: P8).

Benefits planning

As all IS projects should be primarily driven by the host organization's strategic imperatives (Earl, 1993), it was reassuring to find that one of the most commonly occurring benefits planning practices was to review the project's drivers (BP2: identify strategic drivers), to ensure that the project would contribute positively to corporate strategy. However, there was a tendency for these drivers to be expressed in very high level, and often vague, terms such as:

- 'to develop a platform upon which to build new and support existing revenue'(Vision and Scope: P2);
- 'to be a showcase for the use of information technology in government bodies' (Vision and Scope: P4);
- 'to reduce time to market' (Vision and Scope: P8);
- 'to provide improved reporting to enhance strategic purchasing' (Vision and Scope: P17);
- 'to create a new and stable Internet portal which helps the end user to obtain information quickly' (Vision and Scope: P24).

Although this practice (BP2: identify strategic drivers) was widely adopted, it became apparent that it was not being done rigorously. It was as if the project teams knew it was required but did not have the knowledge or motivation required to enact the practice effectively. Although the project aims were typically articulated in strategic terms, there was no explicit discussion of how these aims would be realized, nor any explicit links to corporate strategies to provide evidence of alignment.

Having established the strategic drivers, most organizations had broken these down into a number of lower-level benefits (BP3: identify and define benefits). For the most part these were also ill defined, such as:

- 'reduce the operational costs for maintaining the website' (Vision and Scope: P8);
- 'to provide searchable indexing for website' (Vision and Scope: P20);
- 'to make the work of representatives more effective' (Vision and Scope: P21);
- 'to provide users with easy-to-use online e-procurement for ordering office supplies' (Vision and Scope: P24).

In a small number of cases, there were examples of benefits that were articulated in a more measurable, but not necessarily a business-oriented, form, such as: 'generate 1 million visitors per month' (Vision and Scope: P14). In another case (Vision and Scope: P17), a portfolio of distinct 'business goals' had been established, each of which was supported by a detailed discussion of why it was important, but, for the most part, these goals were expressed in terms of the system's functionality.

By and large, the need to articulate benefits, during a project's planning phase, had been recognized across projects, but all too often these benefits were either articulated in very general business sense, or in terms of the system's functionality and features or its intended usage, rather than in clearly measurable business terms. Moreover, there was absolutely no evidence of organizations explicitly identifying owners for these benefits, to help facilitate their ultimate realization. The difficulty of getting organizations to provide clear measures for benefits was highlighted by a project manager

(P21) who lamented: '*At the start of the project we asked about success criteria and how they [the customer] would measure return on investment. All we could get out of them was that other players in the market already had similar technologies, and they wanted to eliminate all paper from their sales cycle.*'

Even where business benefits are clearly identified, this is not sufficient to facilitate their realization, as the delivery of business value is dependent upon the redesign of business processes, organizational structures and user–working practices, as well as the provision of new technical functionality. However, there was very little evidence from our study that any of the case organizations explicitly addressed these issues in the planning phase of their projects. In a small number of cases, there was recognition that the realization of benefits depended on the changing of business processes. As one report noted: '*one of the biggest mistakes of this project would be to introduce new technologies without changing the processes*' (Vision and Scope: P4). However, there was no evidence of any attempts to establish explicitly the relationship between the redesign of specific business processes with the realization of benefits (BP4: establish benefit-process interactions).

The linking of the delivery of business benefits to changes in stakeholder behaviour was perhaps a little more positive (BP5: establish stakeholder–benefit interactions). Indeed, in one case, an entire section of the functional specification was devoted to detailing: '*the types of people who would be affected by the release, and the manner in which they will interact with the system*' (P14). However, in the vast majority of cases, these analyses focused on the manner in which stakeholders would interact with the system, rather than explicitly detailing how their roles and responsibilities should be modified to facilitate the realization of benefits.

Overall, from our data, the adoption of practices in support of benefits planning is very limited and sporadic. All too often practices are ignored, or where adopted, they typically have a focus on the delivery of features and technical functionality, rather than the realization of benefits. For example, one particularly glaring hole in the case organizations' adoption of practices was the absence of any explicit attempt to formulate a benefits realization plan (BP8: plan benefits realization). Indeed, the main rationale for identifying benefits, in the planning stages of our case organizations, was to facilitate the projects' approval, rather than as a driver for how it is managed. Project teams still strongly prioritize, and focus upon, planning for the delivery of an IT solution, rather than engaging in any systematic attempt to understand the linkage between delivered functionality, complementary organizational change and the ultimate realization of business benefits. One possible explanation for this technological orientation was offered by an interviewee (P6) who noted: *'too many techies were involved in the logical design – there should have been more input from business analysts'*. This view was supported by another project team, where one of the key lessons learned was that: *'to make a successful delivery we need to emphasize the business-driven principle, for the requirements' collection, analysis and prioritization'* (P14: post-implementation review).

Benefits delivery

The empirical data provided little evidence that any of the practices related to the benefits delivery competence were being routinely or uniformly applied. For example, the majority of the projects adopted an 'agile' approach to IS development (BD1: adopt an adaptive project lifecycle), such as that advocated by Boehm and Turner (2004), which might have been expected to facilitate the phased delivery of benefits. However, in practice, it was focused upon features and functions, rather than benefits: *'the release of the solution will be divided into multiple releases culminating in a fully functional, feature-rich solution'* (Vision and Scope: P11).

With the adoption of agile and adaptive development approaches comes the opportunity to make trade-off decisions between different development alternatives, based upon the strength of their relationship to benefits realization (BD5: make benefits-driven trade-offs). For example, in the case of a wide-ranging e-government project, an overriding aim was to: *'find quick win and win-win possibilities and see how the solution can be implemented in the most efficient and quickest way'* (Vision and Scope: P4). However, whilst such approaches were the exception, rather than the rule, at least one other organization realized their importance, albeit in retrospect; as one interviewee noted: *'there should have been more emphasis on the trade-off triangle'* (P6).

One area where there was a little more evidence of practice adoption was with regard to the appointment of a business manager to lead the business change and to facilitate communication with the stakeholder communities (BD2: actively lead the business change). For example, many case organizations appointed product managers or project sponsors, who had a range of responsibilities, including: *'making the final decisions regarding scope, cost and project resources'* (Vision and Scope: P2), or *'defining project objectives and success criteria to ensure that the project remains focused on successfully fulfilling its defined vision'* (Vision and Scope: P20). In another case, a *'technology committee'* had been established, which had responsibility for making *'business-based IT decisions'* (P6). However, in some cases it was evident that the act of appointing business owners or committees had not been translated into any benefits-oriented activity, as was made clear in one post-implementation review: *'the product owner has not been involved in this project'* (P8). Moreover, in many organizations it was clear that the project sponsors had failed in one of their primary roles, namely facilitating communication. As one interviewee noted: *'communications did not always filter down to the teams in a timely manner'* (P6).

All the projects reviewed followed a tried and tested model that proved to be very effective in facilitating the timely delivery of IT solutions, with a small team of fairly technically oriented staff. Unfortunately, there was virtually no evidence to suggest that the project teams had actively engaged in the critical element of benefits realization, namely changes to the design of the host organization, or the working practices of project stakeholders (BD6: implement business changes). Indeed, a review of all the project plans confirmed that no time or resources had been explicitly reserved to enact a programme of organizational change, either before or after systems implementation. This view was supported by the largely negative responses from project managers when questioned about the roles and processes they had in place to manage the delivery of value. Typical responses included: *'from a business point of view, I don't know'* (P13); *'there was no formal role to manage value delivery'* (P21); *'honestly very few'* (P24) and *'not many'* (P25).

Although evidence for the adoption of a wide range of benefits delivery practices from the framework was very sparse, there was one important area in which a new candidate practice emerged, namely, the 'facilitation of knowledge transfer'. Having identified the planned benefits one organization (P8) recognized the need to stimulate knowledge sharing throughout the project, in support of benefits delivery. More specifically, this organization introduced: *'Regularly scheduled, informal briefing sessions, to allow interaction of project personnel and serve as a communication technique for members of the project teams, to provide an effective method of knowledge transfer between individuals and projects'* (Vision and Scope: P8).

Benefits review

From our review of the literature, it was relatively easy to establish a strong case for organizations to develop a competence in benefits review, but there was very little evidence that any specific practices in support of this were being adopted in any of our case studies. In particular, it was rather disappointing that little evidence could be found to suggest that case organizations were neither identifying a set of criteria upon which the success of their projects could be judged (BR1: establish evaluation criteria) nor formally reviewing the benefits realized from their IT investments (BR2: benefits-driven project appraisal). In most cases, the project managers had a clear view as to whether, and which ways, the project delivered value, but they admitted that no concrete evidence had been collected to support these perceptions. Typical responses included: *'no hard value numbers were collected'* (P3); *'it was successful, but I don't think they tried to quantify it'* (P6); and *'there was no assessment in terms of business impact'* (P26). By contrast, in a small number of the cases, specific benefit measures had been collated, using measures such as: *'reduction in unhappy calls to their call centre'* (P5) and *'reductions in the time it took for suppliers to receive feedback on their product sales'* (P25). However, these tended to be very targeted assessments of one or two key benefits, rather than systematic and comprehensive reviews of all benefits. In only one case had a project team attempted to establish a clear link between the original project goals, and the extent to which each had been successfully achieved (P8: post-implementation review).

It was also interesting to note that whilst all 25 of the projects were considered to be technically successful, they were not always viewed as being successful in terms of benefits realized or value delivered. In one notable case, a website for online sales was delivered to a client on time, to budget and to specification. However, within a year the website had been withdrawn as it was failing to attract customers, and deliver any meaningful benefits. As the

Project Manager noted: *'during the dot.com frenzy, value metrics were often overlooked'* (P14). This finding is important as it underlines the point that the successful delivery of an effective IT solution does not guarantee that the resultant system will deliver meaningful business benefits.

Although limited evidence of benefits review practices could be found, there was some recognition that this was a major deficiency, and therefore something should be changed in future projects. For example, one team highlighted the need for: *'better tracking of the complete investment and projected return, in terms of product sales, increased customer satisfaction, service and support'* (P8: post-implementation review). In a similar vein, a project manager noted: *'Return on Investment (ROI) is used to justify projects, but during execution we loose focus on value, and monitoring value'* (P24). If nothing else, this provides some evidence that organizations were reflecting upon the how the performance of the projects could be improved (BR4: conduct review of lessons learned). Overall, however, the general situation was that projects ended at, or soon after, the 'go-live' date for the new software, with project success judged by the on-time, on-budget delivery of a technology solution, rather than through the realization of the benefits.

Benefits exploitation

Because project teams tended to be disbanded soon after the go-live date, there was very little evidence to suggest that ongoing benefits exploitation was explicitly practiced in any of the case organizations. However, in two cases, managers were appointed to have responsibility for the long-term management and performance of the operational software (BE1: ensure ongoing ownership of benefits). For example, one project manager noted that *'after a long battle, we managed to get them to name a person with responsibility for running the complete system – software, people and processes'* (P6). In a similar vein, another organization had explicitly planned to appoint a manager whose responsibilities would include: *'process improvement'* and *'relationships with top managers in various business units and with stakeholders'* (P15: project plan). Whilst in neither case were these individuals explicitly tasked with benefits exploitation, their focus upon the ongoing management of people and processes, as well as technology, put them in an ideal position, to do so.

Discussion: key themes emerging from the analysis of the case studies

The research explored the extent to which a sample of organizations are already adopting benefits realization practices. Analysis of these cases shows that there is a substantial gap between what we know from the literature about the impact of adopting a strong benefits focus (Ward et al., 1996), when managing information systems projects, and what happens in practice. Indeed, the vast majority of the projects investigated for this study focused on the design and delivery of an IT (technical) solution with only a very limited focus on the wider issues of work redesign, process re-engineering, organizational change management and benefits realization. We found no evidence – across the cases – of the adoption of a well-integrated portfolio of benefits realization practices, which could be seen to demonstrate a 'benefits realization capability'. Moreover, although we discovered many individual instances of specific practices being adopted, overall, these practices were not in widespread use, either within or across organizations.

Despite this rather sporadic adoption of benefits realization practices, it was possible to discern a number of important patterns, across the case organizations. For example, it was evident that the focus upon business benefits was most acute at the project's outset: most organizations attempted to identify the strategic drivers for their projects, and then establish the benefits that were sought. However, the rationale for adopting these practices owed more to getting the project authorized and funding approved than it did to acting as a starting point for the proactive management of benefits. Consequently, following their initial identification, business benefits tended to disappear from the project teams' agendas until the software was implemented, at which point the benefits might possibly be evaluated, but rarely in a comprehensive or systematic fashion. The only other significant stage at which business benefits were explicitly considered was during the post-implementation review, during which a number of project teams made clear recommendations that more specific benefits-related practices should be adopted in future projects.

Given that we found very little evidence to suggest that benefits-oriented practices are being adopted in any comprehensive or systematic way, it is important to question why this situation might have arisen. There are at least three plausible explanations to this question. First, as information systems development projects are enacted by a wide variety of human actors interacting in a multitude of ways with a complex technical artefact (De Sanctis and Poole, 1994; Rose and Jones, 2005), there is a high probability that their outcomes and impacts will be exceptionally difficult to predict in advance. There are always likely to be planned outcomes that are not realized (Clegg et al., 1997), as well as a wide variety of unintended consequences (McAulay, 2007; Schultze and Orlikowski, 2004). Consequently, it can be argued that organizations would be wasting their money in trying to proactively manage benefits. A second, or perhaps complementary, explanation might be found in the composition of the sample. It can be argued that consultancy organizations would be very focused on discussing benefits with their clients at the outset of a project, but would then want to be left alone to get on with what they perceive to be the job: delivering a technical solution on time and to budget. Under this scenario, the consultancy would see its job as delivering a solution that has the potential to deliver benefits, but responsibility for managing the conversion of potential into realized value (Davern and Kauffman, 2000) would lie with the client organization, and how they adapt and appropriate their delivered system. However, it is highly unlikely that benefits will ultimately be delivered if the client has not been actively involved in the identification and realization of benefits during the application development phase. The third and perhaps most positive interpretation of our findings is that organizational development teams have limited awareness of the importance of proactively managing benefits, or the availability of benefits-oriented approaches.

Our findings arose because we adopted a practice lens for studying information systems' projects, rather than opting for the more common, and rather discredited, focus upon development methodologies (Nandhakumar and Avison, 1999). Practices relate to how people actually work and may provide an effective way to share knowledge and enable organizations to establish the competences required to realize the potential benefits of IT. We found the concept of 'practice' a useful way to compare how people actually approach realizing benefits from investments in IT, across a wide range of organizations. However, it would be naïve to suggest that the framework of practices could be applied, in an undifferentiated form, in all situations and circumstances. Practices are socially constructed ways of working (Newell et al., 2004), and groups of stakeholders, operating in a particular organizational context, will need to adopt and adapt them to suit their requirements.

Implications for practice

The research has resulted in the development of a conceptual model of a benefits realization capability, enacted through competences and underpinned by practices that explicitly support the effective management of benefits. Unfortunately, the empirical element of the study suggests that very few of these benefits-oriented practices have been adopted in development projects, largely because IT professionals still tend to focus primarily on the delivery of a technical solution, on time, on budget and to specification.

Despite the absence of any clear evidence that it is already being utilized, there are strong grounds to believe that organizations should be looking to establish a benefits realization capability, rather than continuing to pin their hopes solely on the use of traditional systems development methodologies. Moreover, IT should not be viewed and managed as an island, but rather be seen as an integral part of organizational life. Consequently, the establishment of an enterprise-wide, benefits realization capability may have an important role to play in organizations wanting to rise to the challenge of generating value from their IT investments.

From the study's findings, it is possible to distil a number of important lessons that have implications for managers both within and outside the IT organization.

Focus on the benefits, not the technology: For the IT manager, the key message must be that the delivery of a successful technical solution may be a necessary, but certainly not a sufficient, condition for the realization of a range of significant business benefits. Consequently, the outcomes of future information systems projects must be defined in terms of specific benefits to be realized, rather than by the functionality of the technology that is to be delivered.

Effective benefits realization requires ongoing commitment: Having identified the benefits to be delivered, project managers will need to initiate a proactive and ongoing benefits realization programme that ensures that benefits remain the primary focal point for all decisions with regard to the development of the information system.

Benefits realization is a shared responsibility: Because of its strong focus on corporate strategies and organizational change, benefits realization is not an undertaking that can be accomplished by IT professionals alone. Indeed, the primary responsibility for benefits realization should probably reside with managers from the host department, team or business unit that will ultimately own the system. However, IT professionals will need to work in close collaboration with business stakeholders to ensure that the resultant system's functionality and performance are well aligned with the users' needs.

The management of consultancy projects: At a time when the proportion of IT projects being outsourced to consultancies is high and rising (Sauer and Cuthbertson, 2003), there is a need for the customer to be prepared to take on responsibility for the benefits realization activity, as the consultancy may not see this as being within their terms of reference.

For those managers who find the arguments for adopting a more explicit benefits realization approach compelling, our framework of competences and practices provides some very interesting insights into how such a programme might be organized and managed. However, it is important to provide some guidance on how this framework might best be utilized, as we don't want it to become simply another 'necessary fiction', with respect to the management of IT projects. In particular, the empirical study has demonstrated that different organizations have enacted a common practice in their own distinct ways. Moreover, it is unlikely that every identified practice will be needed in all circumstances. Consequently, we would suggest that the framework of practices should be viewed as a reference guide and point of departure for organizations to develop their own benefits realization capability that is tailored to their own ways of working and specific organizational requirements.

5
Succeeding with Benefits Realization

1 case study

Results from an in-depth case study of an organization succeeding with benefits realization and developing the organizational benefits realization capability.

The research

This chapter is a case study of a programme of IT-enabled business transformation at a City Council. The study was carried out as part of a larger programme of research. The case study was one of three in-depth studies carried out to follow-up the 45 initial case studies described in Chapter 4.

I have focused on two aspects of the case. First, factors that contributed to the success of the individual business transformation projects. The case provides a valuable example of a benefits-driven approach to projects of business transformation enabled by IT and highlights a number of insights with implications for practice and theory. Secondly, the case provides insights into factors contributing to the development of the wider transformation capability of the organization. The Council was applying the same approach to the development of the transformation capability as it was to the individual projects. These insights into the practicalities of change and transformation have implications for practice and provide a valuable starting point for further research.

Introduction to the case-study organization

This section provides a brief background on the transformation programme at the Council and the specific projects explored in the research.

The organization involved in this case was a City Council: *'the Council is committed to delivering best value services, which are of high quality and responsive to local views and needs.... improved back office systems and automation of routine tasks will free up staff to spend more time dealing with customer issues ...'* (Council website – 21 July 2005). In 1999, in response to pressure from the government to ensure that local government was providing value for money, the Council undertook a 'best value review' covering IT and various service functions (payroll, council tax collection etc.). The process resulted in extended negotiations to explore outsourcing these Council activities. The negotiations with the potential outsourced service provider showed that savings were possible, but that the service provider would receive most of the benefits. As a result, an internal proposal was developed to match the savings and to allow the Council to take more of the benefits. The result of this exercise was to establish a 'Transformation Programme' that was a three-year plan to drive out savings and invest in improved services. The programme related specifically to the areas of the organization that had been the subject of the outsourcing negotiations, that is the Information Technology department and various Council service departments (IT, Customer Services, Exchequer, Revenue and Benefits).

The Transformation Programme and the related departments became the responsibility of a single director. As part of the formation of the new division, a centralized IT function was formed, bringing together the IT departments that had previously been within each directorate of the Council. The approach taken by the Council very much focused on business change and benefits realization: *'In a compressed period of time we're bringing about radical change in how the Council works using IT as a catalyst... The Transformation Programme plan and the Transformation Programme office is about monitoring the benefits realized and making sure benefits are realized at the appropriate time... IT is recognized as a key business enabler.'*

The case study is based on three projects that were part of the overall Transformation Programme. Table 5.1 provides a brief introduction to the projects. The sponsor of the study, and one of the interviewees, was the Director of the newly formed Council division. Interviewees also included members of the central Transformation Programme Team who managed and supported the overall programme. A number of interviews were carried out for each project

Table 5.1   The three projects examined in the case study

Project	Outline
Desktop renewal	Establishing a 'thin client' desktop system and rolling it out across all 4,000 PCs in the Council.
Human resources and payroll system	The second project was the implementation of a Council-wide human resources and payroll system. Prior to the new system, there were '8 different HR systems and 14 different databases being used by 17 different departments.'
Customer relationship management CRM)	The CRM project was part of a major, long-term pro-gramme to improve customer service: which was about 'challenging the way we operate and delivering services around the needs of the customer'.

and there were additional interviews to explore the overall organizational context of the wider Transformation Programme.

The project to implement the human resources and payroll system was successful: 'the software was installed and data migrated bang on target'. The project involved significant change within the payroll department itself. Some of these changes were directly related to the new system, while others, such as the move from weekly to monthly payroll were business changes taking place at the same time.

The CRM project reduced the need for staff training (from 6 months to 3 months); in particular, time was saved by reducing the need to learn how to use many very different and complex systems. As a result, the service could be provided in local centres. First point of contact resolution of queries rose from 70 to 83 per cent, customer satisfaction improved, with 95 per cent of customers finding the service easy to use and customer numbers increasing from 150,000 in 2002 to 214,000 in 2004 (source: Council website – accessed on 21 July 2005).

Lessons learned: developing competences for successful business transformation

The research has provided valuable insights into how organizations can succeed with business transformation. The case study of the

Council revealed an organization with a clear focus on the realization of benefits rather than delivery of IT solutions. This organization was using a wide range of practices for business transformation. The Council was gradually building what they called a 'Transformation Capability' (i.e. a benefits realization capability in the terms of this research). In this section, I have highlighted some of the key learning points related to each of the competences for business transformation.

Benefits planning

Benefits planning is a crucial stage of a project. I have outlined two of the key findings from the research.

Customer-focused benefits as the goal of the project. Peppard et al. (2007) identify the Benefits Dependency Network (BDN) as a key element of the benefits approach as it links the investment objectives and their resulting benefits in a structured way to the business, organizational and IT changes required to realize the benefits (Ward and Daniel, 2006: p. 133).

The transformation programme at the Council was a three-year change program, consisting of 27 separate projects, each with clearly defined business benefits as the goal. A key part of the approach they took to benefits planning was to seek to identify what was required to make the changes happen and realize the benefits. They found this practice very valuable, in contrast to previous approaches: 'we often had a clear picture about the beginning – "implement a system", and a clear picture about the end – "top quartile performance", but there was a big gap about what goes on in between– "what is the change in the business that is going to benefit the customer"' (C10). The new approach they took to planning each business transformation project filled this gap so that there was a clear understanding of the benefits required, the business changes to realize the benefits and the role of IT as an enabler of change.

The Council illustrates the importance of establishing customer-focused benefits as the goal of a programme or project, and that these benefits need to be the driver for the investment, they need to be clearly defined, well aligned to the stakeholders and the changes required to realize them.

Value of a benefits 'mindset'. The interviewees at the Council consistently emphasized a number of key themes including IT as an enabler; the importance of people and teamwork in project success; and the importance of stakeholder engagement. This consistency was striking. The emphasis seemed to be based on a core set of principles, or common values, guiding the approach they were taking. Factors contributing to this include the fact that a core leadership team had worked together over a period of several years; that new members of the team have been selected, at least in part, based on their fit with this mindset; and constant reinforcement from senior leaders through their involvement in projects and the Transformation Programme.

A key focus at this organization has been to establish a *common language* and shared benefits *mindset* that effectively represent the principles for Benefits Management put forward by Peppard et al. (2007). This mindset represents a 'paradigm shift' (Johnson, 1992) from the technology delivery focus of other organizations.

An important finding that emerged from the research is that a range of practices, for example risk management or phased delivery, can be applied to IT solution delivery or to a business transformation project. The shift from solution to benefits is subtle, for example, affecting those involved and the emphasis taken. Although subtle, this paradigm shift appears to be extremely important. For many practices, the shift from solution delivery to business transformation is more about the new paradigm, or mindset, than a substantial change in the actual practice.

This is an important finding of the research. It has important implications for the adoption of benefits-related approaches and the development of competences for business transformation. All too often, the emphasis of improvement efforts is on the adoption, or perhaps imposition of new techniques, rather than a change of mindset.

Benefits delivery

Benefits delivery is a particularly challenging area. The initial enthusiasm of senior management tends to fade and the focus on business transformation gradually disappears as the focus of the project shifts further towards delivery of a technology solution. The experience of a finance director from one of the Phase 1 cases was typical *'... it was a real shock how rapidly they* [the projects] *each became a technology project – it just happened one after the other. It was really painful'*.

I have highlighted a number of factors that contribute to successful benefits delivery.

Active business leadership. We know that business leadership is important (Ward and Daniel, 2006) and that it is active engagement that counts (Boddy and Macbeth, 2000). This was clearly reflected in the research. One of the project managers at the Council commented on the value of the commitment from their business sponsor at the start of a major change program: *'To get started you could just kick down doors – as we had such strong backing…I couldn't count the times we'd just mentioned…* [the Chief Exec], *this at least got us started.'*

A key factor in the success of a second project was the active role played by the *project sponsor*. He established a clear vision for the project in terms of benefits for the organization and other stakeholders. He played a critical role in realizing the benefits and committed significant effort to the project: *'it took up a lot of time – a substantial number of hours each week for a year. I gave him* [the project manager] *the support he needed'*, he had *'daily contact with the project exec'*. See how this project sponsor described his role in Box 5.1.

Peppard et al. (2007) identify the importance of having business owners of benefits. The research supports this and stresses how active this role needs to be in many situations.

Building an effective team to enable business transformation. Benefits Management stresses stakeholder involvement but not the effectiveness of the project team. The research identified team

---

Box 5.1 The role of the sponsor of a major project

Active engagement of the business sponsor

'My role as project exec was:

- *Challenging of detailed reports.*
- *Co-ordination – handle tensions between different stakeholders, making it happen at board meetings and in between.*
- *Coaching outside the meeting (e.g. other senior stakeholders).*
- *Clarifying roles and making sure people worked as a team.*
- *Anticipating weak areas – for example, at one point, I was concerned out about post-implementation capacity to operate the system and I commissioned a report on knowledge transfer and post-live administration.*
- *Ensuring communication took place and was handled sensitively.*
- *Managing expectations.'*

effectiveness as a crucial contributor to project success. In the words of one of the project managers at the Council: '*Let's just remember that success is about* casting *more than anything else – we could have done the project with different people and it would have fallen flat. It really is about the people.*' '*They were one of the best project teams I've ever had the privilege of working with. This project team was hand picked – I have to say superbly for skills and personalities.*'

During the case study, I identified a range of specific practices that contributed to effective teamwork (see Table 5.2). This helped to illustrate the value of the practices approach as it provided a way to capture and share some of these effective approaches that are not well addressed in traditional project methods.

Building skills for business transformation. An implication of the Benefits Management approach is that business ownership of benefits is essential. This requires extensive business involvement in the projects, for example, through active business leadership. For this involvement to be effective, it is vital that the necessary knowledge and skills for business transformation are available.

One of the initial steps taken by the Council to develop the skills they needed was to provide extensive project management training: '*we established a project management methodology –training has been given to all managers organization-wide – several hundreds*' (CO2). This was later followed-up by further education with a focus on business change. In addition to the education, there was also an

Table 5.2   Examples of practices adopted to enable effective team working

Practice	Definition
Ownership for decision-making	Make individual team members take ownership for making decisions – 'what would you do if you were the CEO?'
Establish project team workspace	Establish a workspace where the project team can be located and work together on a daily basis.
Daily team meeting	At relevant periods of the project, hold brief, daily team meetings to provide a focus for communication and management control.
Adaptive team structure	Adapt the team structure during the project to reflect the changing situation and the expertise and interests of the team members.
Time-box decisions	Use the concept of 'time boxing' to set a deadline for decisions to be made and avoid delays.

emphasis on coaching and supporting, to enable the development of expertise. This was a particular focus of the business sponsor of the overall programme: *'my role includes coaching and supporting.... encouraging and building confidence and a belief in their ability to suc-ceed...talent spotting...management is about releasing the potential of people'* (CO1).

One of the results of this emphasis on education and skills was a focus on effectiveness. It was not just a case of adopting benefits-driven practices – they had to be carried out effectively. The educa-tion and support helped in enabling this.

Education and support contributed to the effective enactment of practices for business transformation and the gradual development of skills in a wide range of individuals across the organization. The Council was succeeding in building the capability to engage in and succeed with business transformation at many levels of the organiza-tion. This was an important output of their overall 'Transformation Programme'.

The emphasis on skills and the effectiveness of the team is a fur-ther important finding from the case study and again shifts the emphasis from the introduction of new benefits-driven techniques.

Benefits exploitation

Benefits exploitation is an important area of the overall framework of competences. In many scenarios, getting the technology in place is relatively straightforward.

From systems deployment to organizational learning. One important perspective on projects is that they are a process of organ-izational learning (Eason, 1988). In many ways, existing project management frameworks are not a good fit with this viewpoint as they tend to focus on the delivery of a fixed solution with the assumption that the definition of requirements and solution is not problematic and can be completed and frozen at the start of a project (Checkland and Holwell, 1998). More recent agile methods recog-nize this issue, although with a focus on software delivery rather than business transformation: 'welcome changing requirements, even late in development. Agile processes harness change for the customer's competitive advantage' (Highsmith, 2004).

One of the projects at the Council was successful, and highlighted some of the challenges of organizational learning that need to be tackled to fully succeed in business transformation. The project had been successful in terms of delivery to time and budget, and many of the benefits were *immediate*, that is the single, lower cost, more reliable system, and there had been good progress in reducing absence. However, there were a number of challenges to consider from the perspective of the project manager that related to equipping the core end-user department to realize the potential benefits. The department was heavily involved in the project: the manager was on the project board, several respected and experienced staff were seconded into the project team. They were also represented in a series of business process re-engineering workshops that explored each sub-process: *'we must have done 70 different processes in the course of the 12 workshops. We invited the business into those workshops, we produced the maps, we produced the end-user procedures, and we produced the training'* (CO4).

Although there had been work on the new business processes, this did little to accelerate the learning: *'they just became flat documents. Unless there's somebody there who truly owns the process and making it stick in the department it just falls flat, and they go through the same period of process discovery that you actually already did in the project. They almost put the manuals and process aside and learn from mistakes. It's kind of what happened – we almost rediscovered the process we'd discovered in a sort of vacuum, by trial and error on the system. So I think there was a real need – once we create a set of documents – to translate those into behaviours – the question is who and how?'* (CO4) Similar issues were seen as they gradually deployed the new system to different teams within the overall department. Each one went through a learning process.

It is interesting to note that on a second project in the same organization a different approach and project team structure was adopted. In this case, over the period of the programme, there had been the opportunity for many of the supervisory staff to develop process mapping and process design skills. This meant that the business team effectively ran the workshops rather than having them 'done to them'. Crucially, this also meant that there was much deeper knowledge of the system and process within the department. The business staff on the first project, outside the core project team, had not had the opportunity to build up the same level of knowledge.

There are significant implications for other organizations. More emphasis on breaking projects into programmes of business change to enable both learning and the development of skills is essential. Also, wider issues of individual and organizational learning need to be a greater focus of project activity. Clegg et al. (1997) suggested that 50 per cent of the cost of change should be allocated to human and organizational factors recognizing the importance of these issues.

Benefits review

For many organizations there are a range of issues to consider related to benefits review. In many cases, an effective review of benefits realized is not carried out. Often this would be impossible, as clear targets were never defined in the first place. In addition, in many cases, benefits are interpreted only as financial benefits for the organization and there is no clear focus on benefits for other stakeholders.

The research provided evidence of a number of important elements of benefits review.

Portfolio-level control of benefits delivery. The Council established an overall Transformation Programme plan, which defined a three-year programme with clear benefit targets. This level of planning provided a strong foundation for managing the programme and for phasing the delivery of benefits. The CRM project, which had started some time earlier, became part of the overall programme and provided a good example of the value of phasing the delivery of benefits: it is now in its seventh year, and each phase, including CRM, has had clear goals and benefits. The organization has not attempted to change everything all at once and have taken time to get benefits at each stage, and also to learn what works and to develop their ability to manage change. The phasing of the programme resulted in a well-defined scope for the CRM project and also meant that previous work had tackled difficult issues of getting other departments involved and starting culture change: They had major challenges in terms of getting the rest of the business on board. I think that's worked to our benefit in the end, because when we have introduced new technology a lot of the business challenges have been tackled. A lot of the culture change was already in progress. I think to try and drive through that culture change and the new technology at the same time would have been a major risk.

There is a clear advantage in taking a portfolio perspective to benefits review. It can help provide assurance of the coherence and achievability of the overall plan, and it facilitates taking a phased approach, which reduces the risk faced by individual projects.

Benefits targets: enabling learning and change. There is a tension between the need for clear benefits in order to get a project approved and the importance of organizational learning, which means that the understanding of the possible benefits is likely to change during the project or programme.

The Council was able to use their portfolio approach to establish a balance between these tensions and challenges. An initial project phase was planned to cover the major costs, for example, of a new software package (payroll, CRM) and provide some direct benefits (headcount, software and hardware costs etc.). Additional phases of work were then planned to capture further benefits; for example, a second stage of the payroll programme focused on the management of absence. The great strength of the payroll project was a willingness to learn: '*so to my mind it was more a process of discovering the benefits and I think it was for the organization as a whole ... they have been superb at scrutinizing themselves and admitting constraints as they learn, but also finding new opportunities as they go through the cycle*' (CO4).

Box 5.2   Factors contributing to the success of transformation projects at the council

- Customer-focused measures of success.
- Benefits mindset: common view of IT as an enabler, and a focus on business transformation.
- Active business leadership of business transformation projects.
- Focus on getting the right people involved to build strong project teams and a focus on developing skills.
- Effective adoption of core project practices (risk management, lessons learned, etc.) with a focus on benefits.
- Education and coaching to develop skills for business transformation.
- Enabling organizational learning as new ways of working are introduced.
- Benefits focus for management of the portfolio of projects – setting priorities and phasing delivery.
- Enabling learning about possible benefits by phasing change in projects within programmes and allowing some flexibility within projects.

Box 5.2 provides a brief summary of some of the factors that contributed to the success of transformation projects at the Council.

Succeeding with business transformation

The Council were also making good progress in developing the 'Transformation Capability' of the organization as an important element of the Transformation Programme. The case study revealed a number of contributing factors.

Gradual adoption of a 'toolkit' of practices with an emphasis on effectiveness

The Director of the Transformation Programme described how when he arrived at the Council he saw a latent change capability in people and the organization. People had been doing the right things but did not know it and were not articulating it as managing change. One of the drivers for the toolkit approach he adopted was to release the potential in people and build on what they were already doing. *'The toolkit is about: standardization; simplification; and sharing. Establishing a series of "tools" is a way to " 'explain what people do" to demystify and make more explicit how to approach change. It provides a way to "make it a common language, a common framework". Working on a toolkit allows people to get involved if they want to help. It provides an opportunity to let people contribute. The toolkit also provides a basis for sharing and improvement and developing a shared understanding'* (CO1)

The customer services manager described their goal as *'making common sense common practice'*. The aim was to keep it simple and build the expertise of the staff so that they can consistently and successfully adopt relevant practices.

The Council used the idea of a 'toolkit' for their collection of practices for business transformation. They gradually developed and evolved the toolkit, linked with the education programme, and the developing experience of the people involved in the projects. They gradually adopted new practices, allowing time for people to learn to use them effectively. The toolkit fitted well with the emphasis given to flexibility and adapting the approach taken to specific projects. It supported the efforts to share learning across the organization and enables incremental development of the transformation capability as new tools are introduced.

Leadership for the development of the transformation capability

The phased adoption of practices for business transformation was part of a wider programme of change to develop the organizational competences required for business transformation. The Council provided an example of an organization with clear leadership for the development of these competences (they referred to a 'transformation capability'). In this case, the same team was also responsible for the delivery of the Transformation Programme and this linkage worked well. Important elements of the approach they adopted were clear targets developed for each project within the overall change programme, developing expertise and capacity for involvement in transformation; establishing a common language; providing a focus on benefits and business transformation; and an overall framework for their approach to projects.

Organizational culture to enable learning

The early steps taken at the Council started to make positive changes to the culture that then enabled further change. Part of their success can be seen in the principles put forward by Lee (1999a) – the instantiation of the new 'intellectual technology', the change framework, resulted in changes to the organization, which in turn affected the further development of the technology. Specifically they found that education based on core elements of PRINCE2, the consistent use of practices including risk management and lessons learned, resulted in cultural changes to allow more open communication and a greater openness to learning: *'Risk and project management training has made us much more receptive to lessons learned – openness wouldn't have happened without project and risk management – we've seen a significant culture change. Identifying risks beforehand and tracking them has been very valuable. We are more aware and receptive. We use risk management. We talk about lessons learned. There is a more open attitude. Management and leadership behaviours have changed – more proactive/constructive'* (CO2). Through the implementation of risk management and lessons learned, they are now more able to be open and honest about what has happened and as a result get insights into what to do differently. Box 5.3 provides a summary of key factors contributing to the development of the transformation capability of the organization.

Box 5.3 Factors contributing to the development of the transformation capability at the council

- Ownership and leadership for development of the business transformation capability, supported by the ability to provide coaching and advice to people involved in project teams.
- Phased adoption of practices for business transformation.
- Phased development of organizational competences for business transformation.
- Adherence to a set of *principles* that represent a focus on benefits delivery. Adoption of these principles will represent a 'paradigm shift' for many organizations, and it is a major issue.
- Establishing an overall project *framework* that provides a basis for the different stakeholders to work together and bring the various competences together.
- An educational programme based on the practices and competences.
- An ability to learn and improve enabled by sharing practices within the organization.

Looking ahead

The high failure rate of projects is not going to be changed overnight after stubbornly resisting all efforts for 30 years. A key starting point for the research was to find a way to make improvements which is a good fit with how people actually work and learn in practice. The idea of organizational competences for benefits realization provides a flexible framework that helps address the organization-wide issues that are involved. The use of the concept of practices has proved to be very flexible, addressing a wide range of issues, many of which are not covered by existing project methodologies.

Developing organizational competences for benefits realization is a process of organizational change that is likely to require a strategic initiative over a period of time. There is likely to be a maturity effect and organizations will need to continue to adopt new practices over a period of time (phased approach) as they gradually develop a benefits realization capability.

There are important lessons for other organizations seeking to improve their ability to realize benefits from projects and programmes of transformation and change enabled by IT.

6
The Challenges of Benefits Realization

This chapter provides insights from a wide-ranging exploratory study to understand how business and IT managers perceived the challenges they faced in building the benefits realization capability of the organization. It also provides an important context for exploring the action required to develop the benefits realization capability of an organization. Thanks to Julie Hodges: an extended and revised version of this chapter is found in Ashurst and Hodges (2011).

The research

In this chapter, I report on the first stage of a longer-term action research programme. I was fortunate to be a member of, and to work with, a forum for IT Directors (ITDF), which operates in the North East region of the United Kingdom. The forum includes representatives from a range of organizations in different sectors and focuses on sharing knowledge to enable individuals and their organizations to realize value from IT and IT-enabled business change.

The members of the ITDF found that the focus of the research on 'benefits realization' was helpful in shifting the attention away from technology. In particular, it is about delivering and sustaining value to internal and external stakeholders and improving organizational performance through benefits-driven IT-enabled change programmes.

The project began in 2008. The first stage included an exploratory workshop with 20 IT directors in April 2008, which provided an opportunity to review key findings from previous research and to clarify the objectives of the research project. Following the workshop, a total of 65 business and IT managers contributed to the data collection interviews. The interviews were transcribed and then analysed using the framework of benefits realization competences as a primary lens. At an early stage in the analysis, I noted that challenges affecting the ability of the organizations to succeed in realizing benefits from IT-enabled change related to individual projects as well as the overall portfolio of projects (investments in IT-enabled change) within the organization. This project/portfolio distinction was adopted to help refine the analysis. An iterative process was adopted to gradually develop an outline of the major challenges.

Following the preliminary analysis of the interview data, we held a second workshop to review the major findings with members of the ITDF. Approximately 20 people attended this workshop. This was an important stage in the research process, allowing the researchers to clarify and refine the findings. A report aimed at ITDF members was then produced with a detailed discussion of the findings; this chapter builds on that work. Ashurst and Hodges (2011) report on this research project.

Findings from the research

The framework of competences for benefits realization (Ashurst et al., 2008) was used as an explicit mechanism for exploring the issues identified by the participants in the research. The framework of specific practices for benefits realization (Ashurst et al., 2008) also provided support for analysing and exploring the nature of the competences, but I have not attempted to present our findings at the practice level, as it would not be possible within the scope of this chapter. I also worked directly from the data and identified broader themes raised by the participants that were related to the development of the required organizational competences.

In this section, I first consider the drivers for change in the participant organizations and then explore a number of challenges faced by organizations seeking to develop their benefits realization capability.

Drivers for change

There is consensus in the literature that change, being triggered by internal or external factors, comes in all shapes, forms and sizes

---

Box 6.1   Drivers for change

'*Our drivers are innovation, creativity and speed to market*' (IT Manager, SME company).
'*Drivers include cost reduction, improved reliability, best value, better service to customers*'(IT Director, consulting services).
'*Compliance is a big driver for change ...* [as well as] *alignment with corporate policy, systems and systems*' (IT Director, public sector).
'*We need to get more value from investment in IT ...*'(IT Manager, higher education).
'*To innovate ... and for speed ... enabling the business to provide what the public want*' (IT Manager, public sector).
'*To enable the use of IT to achieve strategy ... resource costs are too high and need to be reduced*'(Senior IT Manager, education sector).
'*Cost reduction, improved reliability, access to more advanced services ... improved communication and improved processes*' (IT Director, profit sector, June 2008).

(Balogun and Hope Hailey, 2004; Burnes, 2005). External drivers might come from the economic, social, political, technological and legal environment in which an organization operates. For example, the crisis in the financial markets in 2008 resulted in the nationalization of several banks and the merger of others. Internal drivers include the structural, cultural and political environments through which ideas and actions for change proceed (Pettigrew, 1985).

Data from the study indicated that the key drivers for change were to address the dynamic, competitive environment and sustain competitive advantage. In the public sector, compliance with government directives was also a major theme. See Box 6.1.

Benefits review: measuring success

The benefits review competence can be defined as:

> the organizations ability to effectively assess the success of a project in terms of the potential benefits, the delivered benefits, and the identification of the ways and means by which further benefits might be realized. (Ashurst et al., 2008: p. 356)

The benefits review competence includes, but is not limited to, post-project evaluation of benefits. We know from much previous work on IS evaluation that organizations do not carry out these reviews consistently or effectively. Our findings support this:

> *Post-project reviews are not carried out.* (Business manager, financial sector)
>
> *We need to increase benefits by focusing on post-project evaluation and to tie this together across different budgets and cost centres … effective measurement is a key issue.* (Senior IT manager, education sector)
>
> *A key issue is … the lack of evidence of the benefits of changes and more effective ways of working … We know what to do but are continuing to make the same mistakes.* (IT manager, public sector)

Participants referred to a number of specific challenges. First, business case decisions *'don't measure all relevant costs and benefits'* (Director, IT services provider). In addition, decisions are made without taking into account relevant information about what is possible or the wider opportunities across the portfolio of projects within an organization. One interviewee provided a clear example: *'one project had specified a specific low cost router. A second project needed a higher specification – they refused to take advantage of the cross-project opportunity. The first project went ahead with the low cost solution (£50) and the second project then replaced the kit'* (Director, IT services provider).

One interviewee reported the success of a post-implementation review and highlighted that how it was conducted was at least as important as the fact that it took place: *'a very positive factor was that the post-implementation review was fair and objective – it highlighted the issues with each area involved and did not just point blame at IT, it was a mature approach to review and learning'* (IT Director, higher education).

Perhaps prompted by the interviews, a number of participants voiced the need for measures of the benefits realization capability of their organization. No organization had a set of measures in place.

Benefits planning: taking a broader view of change

Benefits do not emerge as if by magic when the new technology is introduced. Benefits come when *people* do things differently and when IT-enabled business change has been planned to realize benefits for customers, staff, the organization and other stakeholders relevant to the scenario. We define the benefits planning competence as:

> the ability to effectively identify and enumerate the planned outcomes of an IT development project and explicitly stipulate the means by which they will be achieved. (Ashurst et al., 2008: p. 356)

The challenge is not just planning for benefits. The focus of project delivery needs to shift from IT implementation to making the changes that will realize the planned benefits. We define the benefits delivery competence as:

> the ability to design and execute the programme of organizational change necessary to realize all the benefits specified in the benefits realization plan. (Ashurst et al., 2008)

A number of participants were struggling to deliver IT solutions effectively. Others were trying to move towards a benefits-driven approach. One participant saw the next challenge as moving to a more agile approach, which would allow faster delivery and also a greater ability to evolve a solution through user engagement during the development process: '*We are taking a very much 80:20 approach. It's like an architectural approach to building a skyscraper – you can dig a hole, pour the concrete, and establish the steelwork before all aspects of the design are finalized – it's a staged freeze*' (IT Director, pharmaceutical).

A key topic raised by the participants is the need to take a broader view of change and not simply to focus on the business process impacts directly related to the system; you have to consider '*what is the change in the business that is going to benefit the customer? Then you have to look more broadly: technology – how is it exploited? People – how are the people engaged? Processes – how are the processes going to change? We also consider communication, training, and culture change*' (Business Transformation Manager, public sector). Participants identified the need to take different approaches to change to deliver the intended benefits: '*We need different approaches to change – e.g. Teaching and Learning needs transformation, Research requires more incremental change*' (IT Director, higher education). Participants highlighted that taking a broader perspective on change would have implications on the skills of the people involved and would need a significant expansion of the IT project toolkit. It also requires a broadening of the skills involved.

In a range of situations organizations will also need to think harder about what they are changing and why. A lot of change is top-down to achieve a single, organization-wide system, process or chart of accounts. One participant provided some powerful examples of problems with this approach: *'corporate level justifications tend to be woolly; one project had a $17m corporate budget and was going to cost $1.2m to implement locally. In the end, we did the whole thing locally for $660k. Very often it's centralization for the sake of it. Is it really worth making the change given all the costs? Is it good enough? It might be better to have simpler, local systems at low cost – not common systems with lots of overhead from Group. Corporate teams become a bottleneck. There is also a focus on best practices – but often this comes from a very large site in the US – their needs and what makes good practice is very different – e.g. they have a site with 5000 people where we might only have or 500 or even 50'* (IT Director, pharmaceutical).

Benefits exploitation: sustaining benefits realization

We define the benefits exploitation competence as:

> the adoption of a portfolio of practices required to realize the potential benefits from information, applications and IT service over their operational life. (Ashurst et al., 2008: p. 356)

In many organizations, benefits exploitation from investments in IT is mainly left to chance. One major issue is that of ongoing provision of education. How do new staff learn about the possibilities of the new system and how can they use it to realize benefits? Very often, this is left to chance: *'end users of systems lack knowledge – it's a case of loss of knowledge through staff turnover and passing on knowledge informally from one to the other'* (Business manager, financial services). The knowledge of what is possible and how to use the full potential of the new technology is quickly fragmented and lost. When many organizations are still using systems 20 or more years old, retention of knowledge to enable continued benefits exploitation is important.

A second major issue is that the initial training is only a start. What provision is there for ongoing learning and the realization of further benefits? 'MIS involves information technology as a form of *intellectual* technology.' Information technology is an intellectual technology not an industrial technology in that it has properties that are not fixed on implementation but can be 'innovated endlessly, depending on its interaction with the intellect of the human beings who implement and use it' (Lee 1999a: p. 8). This can lead to an ongoing cycle of innovation and change as the technology extends the intellects of its users leading to further innovation. Unfortunately, participants did not have a management framework in place for realizing benefits from any significant investment in IT through a long-term process of learning and change. They recognized that they were missing the opportunity to gradually realize the full potential of a system over time as individuals and teams explore what is possible and how they can realize benefits.

Benefits planning: managing the benefits realization portfolio

Previous work on realizing benefits from investments in IT-enabled benefits realization has largely focused on specific projects and programmes. Participants raised a number of issues related to the overall *portfolio* of investments.

In many organizations, there are many opportunities for action. Some are still trying to identify current projects and then to establish a basic framework of controls over the portfolio of projects. The portfolio perspective allowed one organization to deliver rapidly and incrementally: *'delivery was phased – earlier plans had been very broad and ambitious – this project tackled a well-defined area and a small number of staff'* (Operations Director, higher education).

Others have established control over a benefits-driven portfolio of IT projects and are now trying to incorporate all investments in change across the organization into the portfolio, and to establish a more strategic approach to management of the portfolio with strong engagement from senior business management:

> *We need a broader planning mechanism to bring together the various initiatives so there is a wider portfolio and we do not have separate Estates/HR/IT initiatives. We need a broader planning process which is top down and bottom up not just a budgeting process.* (IT Director, higher education)

> *We are now trying to move from local, incremental change to organization-wide transformational change. The cross-organization changes also mean ownership is very difficult – it's either everyone or no one.* (IT Manager, public sector)

One IT Director (higher education) noted that business culture was going to be a significant factor (barrier) in benefits realization as business areas, both academic departments and support departments, were not used to taking an organizational view: *'attitudes/ behaviours are an issue – there is a real focus on the local situation not the wider issues of the university – which may become serious as we start to drive the change programmes.'*

Participants also noted the challenge of managing a portfolio of change projects within different organizational units. Without imposing a vast bureaucracy with central control of every single project, there needs to be a framework that scales up and down so different teams, departments, business units and others can manage local projects as well as their engagement in centrally driven projects.

Building the capacity for benefits realization

The participants raised the issue of the organizational capacity for benefits realization: *'there is a huge appetite for change – the capacity to deliver and absorb is less'* (Head of IT, IT company). Capacity in terms of IT solution delivery and capacity to absorb change was an issue: *'we do not have a basis for planning based on capacity of the business to manage and absorb change'* (IT Director, higher education).

A wide range of factors were identified as affecting capacity:

> *We lack documented business processes and controls, so hard it's to know what you are changing.* (Business manager, financial services)
> *We need to work better together – we work as separate departments. We need to enable better sharing of knowledge and experience.* (IT Director, higher education)
> *Recognition and reward is an issue.* (Operations Director, higher education)
> *There are windows in the year when we can't make changes – Jan to May is payroll year-end and we are too busy. Then it is half year and then it is Q4. We have a change freeze in these busy periods. How can*

you deliver change throughout the year? We need confidence that we can do it. (Head of IT, IT company)

In addition there are many planning issues that impact the effective capacity of the organization; for example, a lack of clarity about what to change: *'a key challenge in a fairly federal organization is to be clear what processes to standardize/centralize and what to leave local. There is a perception that the requirements of each department are different – but perhaps not awareness of the commonality'* (IT Director, higher education). This issue of capacity appeared to be a critical one for the participants, and it requires further consideration.

Skills and knowledge: building the competence of individuals

Let's just remember that it is about casting more than anything else – we could have done the project with different people and it would have fallen flat. It really is about the people. They were one of the best project teams I've ever had the privilege of working with. This project team was handpicked – I have to say superbly for skills and personalities. (Project manager, public sector)

Many participants emphasized the importance of the skills and experience of the individuals involved as a (or *the*) critical factor in the success of benefits realization initiatives. One IT Director (higher education) provided a representative summary of the current situation: *'we seem to have skills gaps, possibly major ones.'*

In some organizations, individuals are recognizing the gap and making the case to attend PRINCE2 or Managing Successful Programmes education. In a few others, a more strategic investment in education was being made. In one, all managers had taken part in a programme covering core aspects of project management including risk management and lessons learned. It would be interesting to assess the value of this education in planned approaches to change and to consider the potential for education taking a broader view of approaches to change.

One organization was going beyond education to establish a framework for ongoing coaching and support to staff to help them gain experience. They also emphasized that they were focusing on ensuring that their 'top talent' was released to take part in benefits realization initiatives and that there was also a career path for business staff who became involved.

Discussion: key themes emerging from the research

This research project has made a number of contributions. First, the qualitative empirical study has provided an insight into the current benefits realization capability of organizations and the challenges they face in further developing this capability. Appendix 3 provides a brief summary of the findings.

There are a number of areas where there is a significant knowing–doing gap (Pfeffer and Sutton, 2004), and current practice does not reflect either the results of research or what the practitioners recognize as good practice. These areas are very much in line with the findings of previous research. We have also identified a number of challenges, for example, related to management of the *portfolio* of benefits realization initiatives and the development of the organizational *capacity* for benefits realization that are not emphasized in previous research.

Secondly, the findings provide support for the proposition put forward by Eisenhardt and Martin (2000) that routines are similar across organizations. The two practitioner workshops provided strong support for the value of sharing practices (routines) between organizations and helped to refine the broad maturity profiles that emerged from the findings (Appendix 4). In addition Eisenhardt and Martin (2000: p. 1117) suggest that the 'order of implementation can be critical'. Our findings support this and suggest that there is a broad pattern of development, which is recognizable across a range of different organizations. A 'maturity model' emerged when developing the findings with the research participants at the second workshop, with a number of different stages of maturity in relation to the different aspects of the benefits realization capability. This model provided a structure for the practitioner report of findings. Appendix 4 provides an outline of the different maturity stages suggested by the empirical data. I present this as an initial framework, which emerged through the research process, and it was found to be helpful by the practitioners. An organization is likely to be at different levels for the different factors. Participants were typically at levels 1 or 2. It seemed that organizations understood their current situation well and could understand the need to move to the next level. Further levels of maturity were tackling 'questions they were not yet asking' and were typically not seen as a priority or relevant. For example, an organization at level 1 would understand level 2 and would probably be aiming to get there, but levels 3 and 4 might be hard to understand and lacking in relevance. The maturity model needs refinement and further research to test out its value to organizations as a diagnostic and planning tool.

The focus of the research on 'benefits realization' was found to be helpful by the participants in moving attention from technology to business issues. The emphasis on developing the benefits realization capability of the organization was also helpful in moving the debate to the intended outcome; that is, the ability to change. A key finding was the desire to adopt a greater range of approaches to change. From a theoretical perspective, this reflects recognition that a planned approach to change is not necessarily the best approach in a specific situation, and the need to address the complexity of the organization when considering what needs to be changed.

A third contribution of the research, emerging as we immersed ourselves in the data and ongoing interaction with the participants, is to establish a revised perspective on how a competence can be conceptualized within an organization. A number of themes, related to the nature of a competence, kept occurring in the interview data. We felt these themes were not adequately reflected in the descriptions of an organizational competence that we had identified in the literature review. An improved understanding of a competence will be important as we move into later stages of the research and work with organizations seeking to develop the competences required for benefits realization.

Figure 6.1 sets out the major perspectives on a competence. It shows the competence existing inside the 'black box' of the formal organization represented by structures, roles and processes. We emphasize three new factors, which build on previous work, and in particular, the framework put forward by Ward and Peppard (2002: p. 180). First, the *paradigm* or principles. At one of the participant organizations there was a shared understanding of 'IT as an enabler' which, along with an emphasis on the skills of individuals, underpinned their development of competences for benefits realization. This contrasted with a second participant organization where the

Within the 'black box' of the formal organization: aspects of a competence

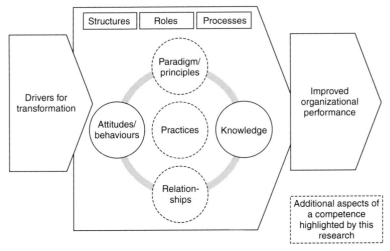

Figure 6.1 Illustrates important aspects of a competence – within the formal organization. A number of competences contribute to the overall benefits realization capability.

In the diagram and the discussion, I emphasize the three aspects not highlighted in previous work (e.g. Peppard and Ward, 2004), that is paradigm, practices and relationships.

Figure 6.1 Competences – within the 'black box' of the formal organization

focus was on introducing benefits-related practices but without a change in the technology-centric paradigm or an emphasis on skills. Adoption of benefits-focused approaches to IT is a 'paradigm shift' (Johnson, 1992) in perspective. Making this shift is potentially a significant challenge for individuals and organizations. An important finding that emerged from the research is that a range of practices, for example risk management or phased delivery, can be applied to IT solution delivery or to a benefits realization project. The shift from solution to benefits from IT-enabled change is subtle, for example, affecting those involved and the emphasis taken. Although subtle, this shift appears to be extremely important. For many practices, the shift is more about a new paradigm, or mindset, than a substantial change in the actual practice. There is also a potential bonus that once the shift in perspective is made, a lot of what is already known is very valuable in the new paradigm. This potentially has important implications for the adoption of benefits-related approaches and the development of competences for benefits realization.

I also noted the importance of **relationships** as a crucial element of the required competences. These relationships contribute to the social capital that Peppard (2007) notes is a vital ingredient of successful benefits realization. In virtually all organizations, there are different groups with their own ways of working and cultures. Often there are considerable barriers between different groups that affect their ability to listen to each other, to understand each other, to value each other's skills and to work together effectively. In many cases, there are big gaps of culture, language, communication and perhaps credibility between IT and other business function and between IT and top management (Peppard, 2001; Taylor-Cummings, 1998).

Unfortunately, in the context of benefits realization, this is a critical issue. The realization of benefits from IT-enabled change requires IT to be effectively engaged with the business at all levels. The alternative is that some other function takes the lead in relation to benefits realization and the role of IT does become limited to technology delivery. The key implication is that IT needs to build truly effective relationships with each business area and with top management.

In addition, we emphasize the importance of **practices** in developing competences (Ashurst et al., 2008). Our findings support the proposition that practices (routines: Eisenhardt and Martin, 2000) are shared between organizations. This provides an important finding and a starting point for further research.

The revised view of a competence (Figure 6.1) appears to provide a more complete view, which will be important as a basis for further research and for action within organization to develop these competences.

Looking ahead

I have provided empirical evidence, based on rich qualitative data, of issues faced by organizations as they try to develop and enhance their benefits realization capability, and, in particular, as they try to realize benefits from investments in IT-enabled change. Several of these issues are not effectively covered by previous research. It was very encouraging to see practitioners grappling with issues that are important from a research perspective. At the same time, the gap between existing theory and management practice provides an opportunity for a contribution to practice in participating organizations by sharing existing knowledge rather than having to wait for the results of further research. I have also provided support for the proposition that there are shared practices across different organizations and there is a maturity effect as organizations adopt new practices over a period to gradually develop a benefits realization capability.

The research raises a number of questions, which provide starting points for further research. In particular, do the drivers for change require different competences? How can the maturity model proposed as an output from this research be refined to provide a resource for organizations seeking to develop their benefits realization capability? Does the revised model of an organizational competence (Figure 6.1) provide a good starting point for the development of organizational competences for benefits realization? How can work on dynamic capabilities inform the development of research on the benefits realization capability of an organization?

7

Benefits Realization from the IT Portfolio

Many aspects of benefits realization relate to management of the IT portfolio rather than individual IT projects (e.g. which projects to invest in). The chapter provides a portfolio perspective on benefits realization competences and practices.

Portfolio perspective: a critical element of the benefits realization capability

Practices for the management of the IT investment portfolio emerged as a crucial theme at an early stage of the research programme (see Appendix 1 which provides an outline of the programme). Participants in the research projects provided many examples of how taking a portfolio perspective resulted in improved benefits realization.

The IT Strategy Director of a financial services company highlighted one of the major barriers to benefits realization: selecting the right projects. She and her business colleagues were unable to get approval for a number of projects that they agreed would enable business innovation and would help the organization exploit new business opportunities. The rigid, cost–benefit approach to investment appraisal adopted by the organization meant that these projects could not be approved, as there could be no confirmation in advance of the potential benefits from innovation. We will never know what the benefits to the business might have been if they had been able to follow-up these opportunities for innovation within the IT project portfolio.

The IT Director at a public sector agency gave one example of saving $600k through the initiative of one of his project managers taking a cross-organization view of the project portfolio. The project manager was given the job of kicking off a new project – starting to establish requirements and building engagement with key business stakeholders: the budget for the project was $600k. She had worked for the organization for some years and had good connections. As a result, she quickly discovered a second project, not connected with the IT function, that was tackling the same issues with a similar budget ($600k). Through the initiative of the project manager, and the influence of the IT Director, the result was a single, combined project with budget of $600k – hence the saving of $600k.

A number of organizations highlighted a third opportunity for benefits realization: from better exploitation of existing systems and information. They had all made substantial investments in enterprise systems, yet there was no investment in continued exploitation of these assets other than reactive help desk and support services. The result, with changing business requirements and the impact of staff turnover, was frustration at the perceived lack of information and lack of flexibility of the systems. One IT Director told us how he had been met with the complaint that 'SAP does not provide the information I need' from a senior business manager. Fortunately, the IT Director had a good knowledge of SAP and did not believe this. He found the right person in his team and had the information available for the business manager the next day. This is just one example of the significant cumulative impact of the lack of knowledge and resulting lack of exploitation of these enterprise systems.

Recent work has provided a definition of IT portfolio management:

> *a continuous process to manage IT project, application, and infrastructure assets and their interdependencies, in order to maximize portfolio benefits, minimize risk and ensure alignment with organizational strategy, over the long run.* (Kumar et al., 2008; my emphasis)

However, previous studies do not explicitly set out the competences and practices that are required to facilitate the management of benefits across a portfolio of projects.

My aim as a researcher was to make a difference and specifically to contribute to the ability of organizations to realize benefits from their portfolio of investments in IT. As a result of discussion with the sponsors, and taking account of my previous research, the following two objectives were defined:

- To identify practices which enable more effective realization of benefits from management of the IT project portfolio.
- To explore how senior managers can approach developing the IT portfolio management capability of their organization.

My focus in this chapter is on the realization of benefits from the portfolio of investments in IT across an organization. The focus on the IT portfolio highlights crucial issues that are not visible when looking at individual projects, or when looking at more general perspectives such as IT governance. To increase the benefits realized from IT, top management needs to focus on practices for management of the IT portfolio. I have set out a number of management practices that contribute to improved benefits realization. I also identify a number of steps that can be taken to improve the IT portfolio management capability of the organization.

There are at least three compelling reasons why an explicit portfolio perspective will enhance the benefits realization capability of an organization:

1. Selecting which projects to invest in is crucial as 'the greatest gains come from doing the right things' (Earl and Feeny, 1994).
2. Benefits often stem from a number of related projects, rather than a single project.
3. Benefits realization practices need to be nurtured across an organization's complete IT portfolio.

A framework for the IT portfolio

An important starting point for realizing value from investments in IT is the IT and Change Portfolio (Figure 7.1: based on Ward and Peppard, 2002, and McFarlan, 1981). This describes the investments in applications and services (those already in place, those planned and future possible applications), not in terms of technology, but in

	Strategic	Exploratory
Transformational change/doing new things	*critical to* achieving strategic objectives	*may be important* in achieving future success
Improving the current business	critical to existing business operations	*valuable but* not critical to success
	Core operations	Support

Figure 7.1   The IT and change portfolio building on Ward and Peppard (2002) and McFarlan (1981)

terms of their role and contribution to business performance. The portfolio enables senior business and IT managers to work together to get a clearer focus on doing the right things: setting priorities and ensuring strategic alignment of investments in IT-enabled change.

There are four classes of contribution to business performance. Core Operations systems are those where the IT is so embedded and necessary that if the system failed the organization would suffer extensively, for example an airline booking system. In any given industry or sector, the organizations within it will have more or less the same Core Operations portfolio.

Support systems focus on efficiency improvement, and its failure does not have far-reaching consequences, for example training records unavailable for a week. Eventually, of course, if the records remained unavailable for a significant period, troubles would occur.

Strategic and Exploratory are quite different – they both concern themselves with the future. Strategic systems are not just very big systems – they are those that genuinely contribute to the business's plans and strategies. When these are implemented, people will work in very different ways – ways that will confer a competitive advantage, for instance. The system does not deliver strategic benefit – that comes from the change in the way business will be done, but the system is nevertheless crucial to the business change, for example integrated international supply chain systems needed for truly global operation.

Exploratory investments are entrepreneurial IT activity, for example prototypes and pilots, of ideas that may confer large benefits. These projects are the basis for innovation. The uncertainty means that large sums of money should not invested until some preliminary business experimentation has taken place to explore if the benefits really exist and how they can be realized. The staged investment of a venture capitalist is the approach to take for these investments. Social media (Web 2.0) is a recent area where an exploratory approach has been a good fit for many organizations.

In a business value sense, the portfolio charts the benefit life cycle of an IS investment: a promising idea is tested for proof of benefits as an Exploratory activity; if it is worthwhile, it is implemented and confers strategic advantage. Because it is good, it is followed by the industry and thus is classed as Core Operations. In time, as better IT offerings emerge, the application may migrate to support.

The portfolio can be used to help to review current IT systems and services; to manage current projects; and to explore priorities for

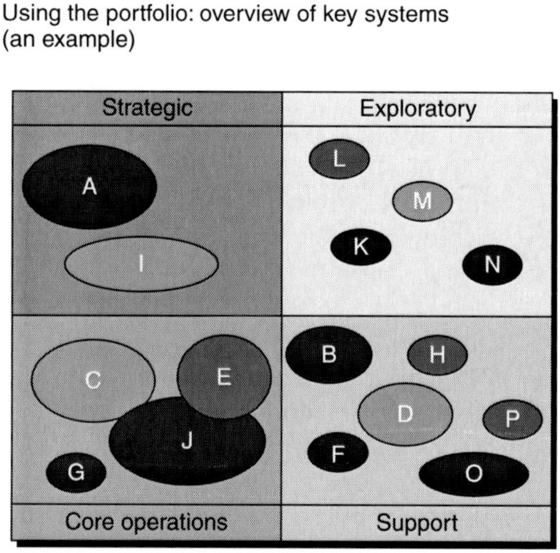

Using the portfolio: overview of key systems
(an example)

Figure 7.2 A portfolio-level perspective of IT systems within an organization

future investments in IT. It provides a very powerful basis for bringing together senior business and IT stakeholders to make informed decisions based on a common, business-oriented language. Figure 7.2 represents a portfolio-level perspective of IT systems within an organization.

Practices for benefits realization from IT portfolio management

In this section, I present a number of key practices for benefits realization from IT portfolio management that were identified during the research. I focus on practices that are of broad applicability and where I have a high degree of confidence in the practice. The practices embed the IT and change portfolio in the management of an organization and tackle crucial factors in benefits realization. Box 7.1 provides a summary of the practices.

I am not presenting a portfolio management 'methodology' or 'maturity model'; the practices simply provide elements of a 'toolkit'

Box 7.1 Summary of practices for IT portfolio management by competence

Benefits planning

(1) Developing winners: shared management of a pipeline of opportunities.
(2) Portfolio-based criteria for investment appraisal.
(3) Setting priorities: taking a long-term view.
(4) Ring fence funds for Exploratory projects.

Benefits delivery

(5) Governance framework: achieving effective control of the portfolio.
(6) Portfolio perspective on benefits-driven projects: emphasizing people and skills.
(7) Managing applications across the portfolio.

Benefits exploitation*

(8) Benefits review of operational services

*Participants identified benefits exploitation as a priority – but I did not identify well-established practices in this area.

Benefits review

(9) Portfolio review – maintaining alignment and control.
(10) Managing risk – taking a portfolio perspective

---

for benefits realization that is a basis for improvisation and adaptation within organizations. I expect the toolkit to evolve, based on experience, as new practices are identified and further evidence emerges of what works in specific situations.

Benefits planning

At one organization the lack of agreed IT strategy was seen as an issue by both the senior management and the staff in the IT team:

> *we've had a few attempts at developing an IT strategy – we still don't have one that's approved – we need more buy-in from the business.* (IT Project Manager)

A director emphasized the importance of planning at a portfolio level, and that it was an area not yet successfully tackled by his organization:

> *the key is to have a balanced portfolio – it's not easily done, and it's not done at all here.* (Business Development Director)

A number of other participants took the view that existing systems and services were satisfactory and that the priority was to focus more of the investment in IT on business innovation and change.

A key aspect of benefits planning is the strategic alignment of the project portfolio, after all 'the greatest benefits come from doing the right things' (Earl and Feeny, 1994). This is the primary focus of the practices I identified.

Practice 1: developing winners: shared management of a pipeline of opportunities

A key concern of many of the participants reflected the need to focus on 'doing the right things'. In any organization, there are many ideas for projects and the ideas with the most vocal sponsors are not always the best. In many cases, there are problems and opportunities that do not develop into specific ideas and proposals because of lack of knowledge of what is possible. There is far too little resource available to work up every idea into a full business case. Therefore, the challenge is to find a way to identify and nurture these ideas and make informed decisions on priorities rather than simply select from the small subset that is pushed forward for consideration.

Organizations tackling these challenges were found to take two complementary steps. First, they had established an opportunity pipeline so that IT and business could work together and explore ideas prior to investment of resources in the development of a full business case. The pipeline needs decision-making gates at a number of stages to filter out less-promising ideas. Some organizations were using very limited seed-corn funds to enable the most promising ideas to be developed further. This idea of using gates is well known but is often only applied to projects in the IT portfolio once the business case is approved. The practice needs to be applied much earlier.

A second focus was based on establishing good relationships so that IT had a 'seat at the table' and were present when business or business unit heads were discussing problems, opportunities or ideas. This is a crucial factor as it enables IT to have an input in terms of what is possible and helps to avoid early rejection of options, or early commitment to inappropriate approaches, that would be hard to change at a later stage. Building relationships is an explicit strategy of senior IT management to get out into the business and explore possibilities, elicit good ideas and manage a pipeline of opportunities.

Practice 2: adopt portfolio-based criteria for investment appraisal

Most participants had traditional, financially based investment appraisal criteria with some form of return on investment formula subject to varying levels of approval, depending on the size of the project. Many participants found this as a challenge, as increasingly projects are required where benefits are not directly financial. This was particularly the case in the public sector (consider improved patient survival rates and patient experience; improved student experience, learning outcomes; increased research impact), but it was not limited to the public sector. The IT Strategy Director at one financial services organization stressed the virtual impossibility of getting projects approved where the motivation is innovation. Consequently, business cases are being adapted to fit existing investment appraisal criteria; for example, estimates of the financial impact of non-financial benefits. In addition, IT investment is being channelled into 'support' projects where it is easiest to establish a financial case at the expense of more strategic and innovative investments.

Participants noted that *people* take these decisions and the investment appraisal criteria are guidelines to help the people involved. It is important to have investment appraisal criteria that would help people to make good decisions. Organizations are now starting to explore a broader set of investment appraisal criteria and to relate these directly to the investment portfolio (see Box 7.2). For example, a traditional, financially based business case is entirely appropriate for a support project. If the same approach is applied to Exploratory projects, none will ever be approved, as the purpose of the project is to explore potential benefits and, by definition, it is not possible to put together a robust business case that is well supported with evidence.

Box 7.2   A broader perspective on IT investment appraisal

Organizations are starting to evolve an investment appraisal scorecard taking into account

Financial measures: any appropriate measure can be used (NPV, etc.). The weighting would be much higher for support projects.

Strategic alignment: the extent to which the project contributes to the strategic objectives of the organization. This could be given a high weight for a Strategic project.

Organizational risk: the business risk related to the business opportunity and the management of change.

Future options: an investment might create a range of opportunities that could be of value in the future – this puts a value on flexibility.

Contribution to architecture: the project may contribute services and/or functionality that are of broader value to other projects.

Technical risk: an assessment of the technology risk.

The different factors are weighted according to the element of the portfolio. Financial measures are the key for Support projects. Strategic alignment is the primary focus for Strategic projects. For Exploratory projects, the key is spreading *limited* funds across a range of promising ideas and getting good learning. Who takes the decisions is also important – for Exploratory and Support projects, there are strong arguments that there should be some element of local autonomy and control, even in what is otherwise a centralized governance framework.

One participant provided an excellent example of the importance of people in the decision-making process and specifically having the right knowledge involved from an early stage. The IT manager stressed the importance of procurement and vendor management and identified major savings that had been achieved:

> *They went out to tender. Z was one of two leading suppliers. They realized they had the whip hand. Z used high-pressure sales techniques – the sponsor and manager had no experience of resisting this. The vendor sent up a lot of high profile people. I stepped in and stopped it. I had to convince the directors. Z threatened to sue. I'd been through it before – it didn't frighten me. I brought in a contract project manager who'd delivered eight of these. We went out to tender again using his experience. They'd tried to oversell us on licenses by £300k. We also saved £300k on services (from £500k to £200k) and we gained flexibility. It was a shame it wasn't sorted earlier.* (IT Director)

Procurement and vendor management are revealed as important factors contributing to benefits realization, and must be managed at the portfolio level as part of the wider investment appraisal process to ensure that the best possible deals can be leveraged from suppliers.

Practice 3: setting priorities: taking a long-term view

A further significant challenge when considering strategic alignment and priority setting is that there is often no single, clearly defined set of priorities. Several participants highlighted how business unit priorities differed from corporate priorities. There was also a strong belief that the public sector faces particularly high levels of uncertainty, which makes the strategic alignment of the portfolio difficult. These organizations are always vulnerable to imposed changes of objectives and to these changes happening faster than they can deliver change programmes.

Participants generally acknowledged the different time horizons of business and IT planning, with IT often needing to consider 3–5 years or more, which goes well beyond typical business-planning cycles. As a result, IT is potentially caught between different versions of business priorities and has to make a case for a longer-term perspective that is not directly aligned to short-term business priorities. Organizations with business control of IT priorities and budgets risk taking short-term decisions with adverse consequences in the long term.

In this complex area, organizations are adopting a number of practices. In addition to building relationships and developing engagement with business strategy and planning processes at all levels of the organization, forward-looking IT organizations are developing an IT strategy including a 3–5 year architecture and technology roadmap so that they are gradually developing a strategic 'digital platform' (Weill and Ross, 2009): *'we're working towards a long-term systems roadmap for each system with academic and non-academic colleagues'* (RUGIT – from workshop with Russell Group of Universities IT Directors Forum).

Practice 4: ring fence funds for Exploratory projects

Seed-corn funds and pilot projects were being used in a limited way by a small number of project participants and represented first steps towards the explicit use of Exploratory projects to enable innovation and to reduce the risk of larger investments. There was a 'skunk works' element to these projects: one IT director admitted that he had to use the stationery budget to fund some initial work on a potentially important project. There was also some concern that any failures might be at cost to the credibility of the IT function and to individual careers, so participants were keen to establish a more entrepreneurial environment.

Organizations need to make use of the concept of Exploratory projects, and acknowledge that some will fail if they are indeed being used in exploratory, high-risk scenarios. Failure would be a good thing, as it provides an opportunity for learning and it avoids much greater losses on a Strategic or Core Operations project. A small element of budget (5% perhaps) is ring fenced for Exploratory projects and a simple selection process is established. Projects tackle interesting areas with small teams and budgets adopting an agile approach (Highsmith, 2004). In many senses, this venture capital approach provides funds in tranches and balances innovation and risk. Table 7.1 provides examples of practices for an Exploratory project.

Table 7.1   Practices for an exploratory project (examples)

Practice	Outline description
Time box	Time boxing is a key practice – working to a deadline for the delivery of each phase and using this focus to enable innovation.
Incremental development/ phased delivery	Totally linked with time boxing is the focus on incremental or phased delivery. It results in smaller projects that are easier to manage, provides motivation for the team and is a quicker route to benefits and learning.
Manage trade-offs	The feature–time–resource trade-off is aligned with the time-boxed approach. The key driver is to deliver, shifting features to a later release if necessary.
Co-located team	The creation of a physical space for innovation can be vital. It allows sharing of tacit knowledge and effective ways of working with a minimum of paperwork and bureaucracy.
Phased funding	A venture capital model is adopted. Small tranches of funding until there is evidence of benefits and the teams' ability to deliver.
Entrepreneurial team	The people are key. An entrepreneurial, multidisciplinary team will make the project succeed. They might break a few rules along the way – just focus on creating the environment where they can innovate and make things happen.

Benefits delivery

The link between strategy and implementation is often weak:

There is a lack of leadership and corporate ownership. What isn't in place is a management framework to oversee the process of how IT should be deployed. We have written a strategy but it needs to be owned by somebody. There have to be priorities, and new requirements have to be considered in the context of the plan. It has to approve projects. The strategy mustn't go in the top drawer; it must be a working document: it needs to be owned and managed. We need a rolling 3–5 year plan for IT. We don't have a governance framework that ties in directorates and IT.(Business Development Director)

Control over existing projects can also be weak. An HR Director gave an example of a lack of control over the portfolio of projects: '*IT*

Projects can bounce along for years and no one has got around to delivering anything.' The IT Manager indicated that there was a clear *'IT attention deficit'* (Huff et al., 2006) contributing to the lack of control:

> *Project X has been going on for three years, I went to the senior management team – they looked bored after five minutes – either you need to understand it or you need to empower me.* (IT Director)

One project manager indicated the impact of lack of planning and control on resource allocation:

> *The trouble is planning, the lack of certainty of dates. I was booked in for a project and it didn't come through for over a year. You get to the point you never believe a word anyone says. No deadlines are ever met. You need to be able to plan properly.*

As a second project manager noted:

> *who knows what projects are being worked on? Who knows where there are overlaps? There would be big benefits if we knew what was going on.*

In this situation, there is no portfolio of agreed projects, and there are no management practices related to the control of the portfolio. As a result, it appears that progress of projects is not effectively controlled, coherence of the projects is not ensured and there is considerable difficulty in resource planning.

Practices addressing benefits delivery include effective governance of the portfolio and a clear portfolio management process.

Practice 5: establish effective portfolio governance

Management of the portfolio becomes a key driver for benefits realization. It provides a link between strategy and implementation. Phased benefits delivery and an agile approach to projects will tend to mean more, shorter projects and a greater emphasis on learning and evolution of plans. The portfolio approach, and specifically the different types of investments, builds in an improved level of flexibility to enable the organization to respond to changing circumstances.

Participants stressed the importance of establishing effective governance structures for the IT portfolio that bring together different stakeholders, specifically senior business leaders responsible for setting priorities and sponsoring change initiatives, with IT and other professionals involved in delivering the change programmes to realize the benefits. In some organizations, this is a challenge, because of the lack of status of the IT function and lack of involvement of the Chief Information Officer (CIO) at the top level.

The governance framework is likely to evolve as the transformation capability develops. For example, a starting point might be to establish effective portfolio-level control over all IT projects. A later stage might be to establish an organization-wide view of investments in change addressing setting priorities (strategy), delivery of benefits through change (implementation) and exploitation of existing systems, services and information.

I also noted that the governance framework must provide scope for flexibility and that the portfolio helps to manage this. For example, *'IT may try to control too much. We created a community approach to mobile applications – drawing on IT provided web services. IT are not supporting the applications themselves'* (RUGIT). The flexibility can allow for different levels of resilience (and cost), but there are barriers: *'Audit Committee take a view that everything has to be resilient. We need to allow different views'* (RUGIT).

It is interesting to note the comment from one participant in relation to a previous attempt at improved governance: *'we tried before but the group wouldn't take the decisions on priorities.'* This emphasizes that, by itself, establishing a new, formal governance structure will not achieve the necessary improvements. Relationships are key, and it is vital to have the right people involved and committed to make it work. One approach is to embed management of the portfolio in existing structures; a number of IT functions had representatives on business unit management teams and were tackling portfolio management in this forum.

Practice 6: take a portfolio perspective on people and skills to drive benefits realization

Benefits are achieved when a project specifically focuses on benefits realization from organizational change and not just from technology implementation. We know that benefits-driven approaches have not been widely adopted and that most projects still have a technology focus. Evidence from the current study suggests that the interaction between the portfolio and the individual projects is a critical opportunity to influence the adoption of benefits-driven approaches and to enable benefits realization.

At project initiation, there is a portfolio-level role in finding the right people to be part of the project team, as well as helping to establish an approach to the project that is effective in the context of the investment portfolio. In the Higher Education (HE) context, capacity for business engagement can be limited: *'there is limited capacity for academic engagement in projects and programmes – not many are willing and able to be involved – so we just pick strategic projects and focus academic leadership on these'* (RUGIT).

For many projects, particularly Exploratory and Strategic, innovation is important. A key question is *'how do we capture the creativity and entrepreneurial spirit that there is in academic depts?'* (RUGIT). One approach is to recognize the need for different contributions and to build a team that brings together the required skills: *'Academics can be entrepreneurs – they tend not to be completer-finishers. IT can provide support. There is a journey from project to service – academics are not geared to provide a service – others need to take the ideas forward'* (RUGIT).

In the design and development stages of a project, the portfolio perspective also helps in consideration of architectural issues. For example, should the project be drawing on existing application or infrastructure services? Should the project be contributing new services that will be used by other projects? Throughout the project, there will be opportunities to share learning with members of other project teams. The source of guidance and portfolio-level control will vary from organization to organization. It may come from individuals in line-management positions (e.g. the Chief Information Officer), or there may be an advisory element to the role of a Project Management Office (PMO). The appropriate model will depend on a range of factors including the experience and management style of the individuals. From a benefits perspective it is vital to ensure there is relevant expertise in benefits-driven approaches in project teams, and that support and advice is available as necessary.

There are a number of additional practices at a portfolio level, such as developing people with relevant skills; getting people with the necessary skills allocated to projects and in appropriate roles; creating a career development framework that encourages the development of benefits-related skills in IT and business professionals and sharing practices for benefits realization. In addition, guidance can be provided on adapting the approach taken to a project based on the portfolio. Although practices in these areas are clear from the 'textbook', I have not yet observed them in practice and have not included them here.

Practice 7: use the portfolio to manage application life cycles

The portfolio helps to explore the management of software applications over time. Most participants in the studies attempted to operate a centralized, monopolistic decision-making strategy related to IT application software. One micro-case study highlights some of the challenges (see Box 7.3).

The case simply illustrates the more general practice that applications need to be periodically reassessed from a portfolio perspective.

Box 7.3 An example of issues in application lifecycle management

Application Lifecycle Management Case Study

A university has a core eLearning system used by 90 per cent of its 20,000 students. It is reliable and effective. However, it looks dated and does not provide Web 2.0 features. A professor in Computer Science has developed a new eLearning system and its usage is gradually growing in other departments. It looks up to date, and it has some clear functional advantages over the core university system. The system is hosted on a server under the professor's desk. It is becoming unreliable as usage grows and no one other than the professor can provide support. The university structure is federal, with individual departments having a lot of autonomy, and individual, successful, professors have considerable freedom of action.

* * *

The investment portfolio helps to identify a number of possible actions in response to the case study. For example, if the new eLearning system is currently Exploratory, there might be an opportunity to move it to Core Operations or Strategic by IT taking on the management of the infrastructure and investing in the core eLearning system to add new functionality to replicate the system. Alternatively, IT could re-engineer the system to provide a sound basis for further development and production operation.

Applications will move around the portfolio as the positioning is related to strategy. The key is to manage the movement so that the implications for management of the application are assessed and, for example, service levels adjusted accordingly.

Benefits exploitation

The participants in the studies identified exploitation of existing systems and information as a top priority. Given the relatively little action actually being taken, I suspect the need to 'sweat the assets' has been brought into sharper focus by the general economic climate.

Existing systems have generally been taken for granted. Often these are major enterprise systems, such as SAP, where post-implementation the emphasis has moved on, leaving a small support capability to resolve specific problems. Participants reported a gradual loss of knowledge from the turnover of IT and business staff, resulting in less of the capabilities of these systems being used and an unnecessary inflexibility in the face of gradually changing business requirements. The loss of knowledge can easily be reinforced due to busyness and bureaucracy, giving the impression of poor systems

---

Box 7.4   Examples of practices for benefits exploitation

- Regular review of system usage, including an annual end-user survey, is carried out to understand satisfaction, identify problems, explore opportunities and to provide input into future developments.
- An annual user conference is held to provide an opportunity for end users to share how they are using the system and for good ideas to be communicated. The IT team provides additional input to the conference, based on their work with the solution provider and attendance at the user-group meetings that include other organizations using the software.
- Regular updates are provided to help guides and training courses that address how to get the most value from the system. Help information is provided in the form of a wiki, enabling broad participation in sharing ideas and advice.
- Consultancy services are provided to end users and user departments by the IT, with the aim of tackling specific projects to help them realize additional value from using the system: *'we'll put in time to run a series of short seminars to provide updates on the new features and then we can work 1:1 with people who want specific advice.'*

---

and a 'can't do' IT function. The example of the IT Director quoted earlier, showing that SAP did have the information required by the senior business manager and that it could easily be made available, shows what a difference attitude and behaviour can make.

There is a view that this is a business issue and not IT's problem. I argue that IT needs to step up and take a lead as this is so important for an organization and the current situation reflects badly on the IT functioning. Box 7.4 outlines a number of specific practices from an organization involved in one of our earlier research projects.

Practice 8: establish benefits owners and carry out a periodic review of operational services

Although I discovered very little evidence of consistent practices related to Benefits Exploitation, one organization was starting to establish what appears to be a potentially valuable practice.

The aim is to have clear business owners (often multiple, to reflect the organizational structure) for a specific IT service (or system/business process) and then to carry out a regular review between business and IT to explore if benefits are being sustained and developed. These give an explicit benefits focus to existing service management practices and aim to take into account the rapidly changing organizational context.

Benefits review

Benefits review highlights a crucial conundrum: everyone knows it is important to carry out post-implementation reviews of projects, yet they are only rarely carried out. The gap between what we know and what we do is a crucial barrier to the development of the IT portfolio management capability of an organization. Portfolio management needs to ensure that these project-level benefits reviews are carried out regularly and that action is taken as a result.

The research provided participants with an opportunity to reflect on lessons learned, which is a critical element of the Benefits Review competence. One IT Director highlighted how the gap between business and IT affected Benefits Planning:

> *The project manager even said to me 'if I can get rid of all this compli-
> cated IT, I can make it deliver'. The project initiation document wasn't*

originally shown to me. It said we will do this bit and IT will do the rest. Like we'll install the ATMs and IT will provide the rest of the bank. The way the PID (project initiation document) was written it was a no-win for IT. I had to beg $20k to do some studies. To start off I had to use the stationery budget.

An IT manager saw the need for shift from technology implementation to a greater benefits focus, for alignment of objectives with stakeholders and for explicit change management programmes to deliver the intended benefits:

There are also things to do about programme management – but we need strategy. Then we need staged projects and stakeholder alignment. Project management is not just about making a machine; it's about transforming the service. For example, the X project was $4m, of which $110k was technology. It involved a huge effort in communication and support. Change management has been a lot more important than the technology.

It is also important to note how a large business project has a small, but critical IT component, which emphasizes the need for the portfolio to encompass all investments in change.

Practice 9: carry out a periodic review of the portfolio to maintain alignment and control

The IT portfolio represents a significant investment in change. It is also a crucial link between the strategy of the organization and the implementation of change. In the absence of a regular review of the portfolio, there is a risk of loss of control over these investments, and the alignment with business strategy may drift as business priorities change.

A key element of control is provided by half-yearly reviews of the overall project portfolio, which are aligned with the business-planning cycle. The reviews, varying between a day and half day, provide an opportunity for an in-depth review of the portfolio. This provides an opportunity to reassess the strategic alignment of projects and to take a broader view of progress and lessons learned.

Initial sessions are likely to identify a range of issues and to help establish an effective governance framework. Although there may be opportunities to consider the different constituents of the portfolio (current systems, current and future projects) in different sessions, it is normally helpful to maintain an overview of the entire portfolio. It is important to take a pragmatic approach to the portfolio and the review process. For example, in some cases it may be necessary to start with the IT function and IT projects. Clearly, the goal is to move to consider all investments in IT-enabled change and preferably all investments in change.

Depending on the size and structure of the organization, the portfolio may exist at a number of different levels (e.g. each business unit and the organization as a whole) and reviews should take place at relevant levels. At all these levels, it is important to ensure that there is knowledge and expertise in portfolio management, as well as effective engagement from the individuals involved.

Practice 10: managing risk: take a portfolio perspective

We know a lot about managing risk on IT projects. Just look at any book on IT project management. Unfortunately, a focus on risks related to a specific project misses most of the big issues; for example, as the 'biggest gains come from doing the right things', risk management at a project level can be about trying to succeed with projects that should never have been started.

Once a portfolio view is established, that is all projects are allocated to one of the quadrants and a core set of information is available on each project, it provides the basis for a much more strategic approach to risk management. For example, *Core Operations* projects are affecting critical business activities – this can be compared to changing the engine without stopping the car. So there has to be a real focus on mitigating risks. *Exploratory* projects are very different. A risk-averse approach would mean that either these projects never take place or they cost far too much. This is the place for innovation and taking risks – but limiting the potential damage by keeping the budgets and resources small. It also means recognizing that some of these projects will fail – and that is ok.

Taking a portfolio perspective is critical to effective IT risk management. The portfolio provides guidance on the attitude to risk on different projects. It also helps to align the overall set of investments in IT with the business strategy – providing a real focus on business opportunities and risk. Risk management becomes a key element of the portfolio management and review process.

Overall picture – a lack of focus on the IT portfolio

My findings provide support for the importance of IT portfolio management as an element of the benefits realization capability of an organization. I have set out a number of specific practices emerging from the research that will help organizations realize benefits from the IT portfolio.

In almost all cases, participants in the research agreed that managing the IT portfolio, as set out here, had not been a top priority prior to their engagement in the research. Practices were established because of specific initiatives and in response to particular problems, rather than as part of a co-coordinated attempt to develop more effective portfolio management.

Previous work on benefits realization from IT has largely focused at the project level. The main contribution of this chapter is to focus on the management of benefits at the portfolio level, and then to identify a number of areas in which portfolio-level practices are emerging and can be adopted to improve benefits realization. The study also contributes to the developing literature on IT competences and capabilities by providing new insights into why it is as important to manage IT projects proactively at the portfolio level, as it is at the individual project level.

Senior IT and business managers wanting to increase the benefits realized from IT in their organization should consider the actions they will take to improve IT portfolio management. I have provided a number of possible starting points in this chapter. The IT Director of a large public-sector organization took a few minutes out to reflect on the progress he had made introducing portfolio management and the challenges ahead.

A key success was to get the 'top 15' list of programmes and projects agreed with the Chief Exec and COO. They immediately saw the value in having this clear focus. We'll use this in the next business planning cycle as part of priority setting. The next step is to get a shared view of how to manage the inevitable changes as business priorities shift and new opportunities are identified.

A second big win was introducing the concept of 'Exploratory' projects – it's really opening up opportunities for innovation. My next challenge is to use the portfolio to help shape the approach to each of our projects, so we give ourselves the best chance of succeeding.

It's been great to see business colleagues using the portfolio model – and not just in relation to IT investments.

8
Building the Capability – Breaking out of the Catch-22

The chapter draws on several research projects to explore the barriers to the adoption of benefits-driven approaches and how they can be overcome. It makes the case that developing a benefits realization capability within organizations needs to be approached as a benefits-driven change programme: that is, they need a benefits realization capability. So organizations are stuck in a catch-22: to succeed in developing the benefits realization capability, they already need the capability they are trying to develop. The chapter sets out some ways forward.

Building an organizational capability for benefits realization

My interest is in succeeding in realizing benefits from investments in Information Technology (IT). Benefits may be for customers, employees, other stakeholders of the organization, for the organization itself and its shareholders. I am following the principles that (1) 'IT has no inherent value' and (2) 'benefits arise when IT enables people to do things differently' (Peppard, Ward and Daniel, 2007, pp. 2–3). This is consistent with the idea of 'technochange' (Markus, 2004), which states that value is realized from investments in IT when the investment is managed as part of a project or programme of organizational change. Value is realized when the focus is on delivering benefits for stakeholders rather than just on delivery of an IT solution.

There have been reports of a 70–80 per cent failure rate of IT projects in terms of benefits delivery over the past 30 years (British

Computer Society, 2004; Clegg et al., 1997). This high failure rate means that billions of dollars are wasted and there are even greater lost opportunities. I consider the reasons for the lack of adoption of benefits-driven approaches to IT investments. I outline the implications for management in organizations, who want to overcome this high failure rate and build the capability of their organization to realize the strategic potential of IT.

Realizing benefits from IT

Stuck in a techno-centric approach

It is widely acknowledged that a considerable amount of time, money, effort and opportunity have been wasted upon IT investments that have either been abandoned or ultimately failed to deliver any appreciable benefit (Ewusi-Mensah and Przasnyski, 1994). Indeed, it has recently been suggested that *'only around 16 per cent of IT projects can be considered truly successful'* (British Computer Society, 2004: p. 8). There is also an established stream of research to suggest that the root cause of this problem is the failure of project teams to consider explicitly the organizational impacts and implications of a new piece of software and to manage proactively the associated organizational change (Clegg et al., 1997; Doherty and King, 2001). Indeed, it has been persuasively argued that benefits are typically leveraged from the changes to organizational structures, cultures, working practices and business processes that accompany the introduction of a new technology, rather than from the technology itself (Peppard, Ward and Daniel, 2007). Unfortunately, the typical IT project team will focus upon the delivery of a technical solution, and only concern itself with organizational impacts once the system is operational (Markus, 2004; Ward and Daniel, 2006).

Against this backdrop, it can be argued that organizations should attempt to break away from their current techno-centric mindset, which focuses on the delivery of IT solutions, on time and to budget. Success will only come from a shift in mindset and practice that recognizes that benefits will be realized only when IT development projects are re-conceptualized as being first and foremost exercises in organizational change which address the perspectives of the multiple stakeholder groups affected (Blake et al., 2010). To achieve this, the boundaries of the IT development project will need to be redrawn, so that the design exercise will encompass all of the complementary resources, processes and activities, with which the technical artefact will ultimately interact, as well as the development of the new IT application, itself (Melville et al., 2004). Although there has been an awareness of the need for a benefits-driven approach to IT investments that addresses organizational changes for some time (Clegg et al., 2007; Doherty and King, 2001; Markus, 2004; Peppard et al., 2007), there has been limited change in what actually happens in organizations. Through my research, I have seen many organizations fail in their attempts to adopt benefits-driven approaches to improve their success in realizing benefits.

Establishing a 'benefits realization capability'

One potentially rewarding way for organizations to change their approach to IT development projects, to ensure that a more explicit focus upon the delivery of value is adopted, and that organizational change is proactively addressed, is through the establishment of 'benefits realization capability'. Such a capability can be defined as the ability of the organization to mobilize the co-ordinated portfolio of practices, competences and skills, necessary to leverage meaningful benefits from IT development projects (Ashurst et al., 2008). However, developing a benefits realization capability is no simple matter, as it requires a radical shift in organizational thinking, and management practices, to break free from the traditional technocentric mindset. The establishment of a benefits realization capability is in itself an exercise in complex organizational change. Consequently, it is not surprising that organizations, which have failed to incorporate effective organizational change management practices into their IT projects, will not have the appetite, confidence or competence to develop this capability.

In this chapter, I aim to describe a 'benefits realization capability' and demonstrate that its successful introduction requires organizations to make an explicit commitment to improving their ability to effectively manage IT-enabled change. I use the results of a major empirical study to demonstrate that it is the inability of organizations to effectively manage organizational change, which is both hindering the realization of benefits from individual IT projects and preventing them from breaking free from their traditional ways of managing IT development projects. I then present the results from one case organization that has been successful in breaking out of the techno-centric mindset, and is currently in the process of developing a very effective benefits realization capability. Finally, I consider the implications for other organizations seeking to increase the benefits realized from their investments in IT.

The framework for a benefits realization capability that underpins this research is set out in Chapter 3.

The development of benefits realization competences

The design of the research project

Having defined a benefits realization capability, I initiated an empirical study to explore the extent to which the projected competences were already being enacted in an organizational context. The research study initially comprised a thorough analysis of 45 IT projects – based upon detailed documentation reviews and follow-up interviews with project managers – in a wide range of organizations in the US, UK, Europe and other locations. In a second phase, I carried out in-depth case studies in three organizations and explored the competences and practices for benefits realization being utilized on three or more projects in each organization. The researchers were able to secure full access to these organizations, and consequently the findings were drawn from a mixture of multiple-respondent interviews, detailed documentation reviews and researcher observations. Having assembled this very extensive and rich, qualitative data-set, it was thoroughly reviewed, to highlight evidence that practices contributing to benefits realization were being undertaken, or more commonly, definitely not being undertaken, and assess the level of each benefits realization competence.

Lack of adoption of benefits-driven approaches

Our qualitative analysis of these 45 project-based cases, and two of the three in-depth cases, indicated that there is a very substantial gap between what we know from the literature about the impact of adopting a strong focus on realizing benefits through organizational change when managing IT projects, and what happens in practice. Indeed, the vast majority of the projects investigated for this study focused on the design and delivery of an IT (technical) solution, with only a very limited focus on the wider issues of work redesign, process re-engineering, organizational change management and benefits realization. We found no evidence – except in the case described below – of the adoption of a well-integrated portfolio of benefits realization practices and competences, which could be seen to demonstrate a *benefits realization capability*. Moreover, although we discovered many individual instances of specific practices being adopted, overall, these practices were not in widespread use, either within or across organizations.

Despite this rather sporadic adoption of practices contributing to benefits realization, it was possible to discern a number of important patterns, across the case organizations. For example, it was evident that the focus upon business benefits was most acute at the project's outset: most organizations attempted to identify the strategic drivers for their projects, and then establish the benefits that were sought. However, the rationale for adopting this approach owed more to getting the project authorized and funded, than it did to acting as a point of departure for the proactive management of benefits. Consequently, following their initial identification, business benefits tended to disappear from the project teams' agendas until the software was implemented, at which point the benefits might possibly be evaluated, but rarely in a comprehensive or systematic fashion. Indeed, once underway, the studied projects typically followed the prescriptions of established systems development methods, which proved to be very effective in allowing small teams of technically oriented staff to deliver technical solutions, in a timely fashion. Unfortunately, there was virtually no evidence to suggest that the project teams had actively engaged in the critical element of benefits realization, namely the enactment of changes to the design of the host organization, nor the re-engineering of business processes or the working practices of project stakeholders. The only other significant juncture at which business benefits were explicitly considered was during the post-implementation review, at which stage a number of project teams made clear recommendations that more specific benefits-related practices should be adopted in future projects.

Barriers to development of the benefits realization capability

In addition to discovering that there was remarkably little emphasis on benefits during the conduct of systems development projects, this

Table 8.1   Barriers to the development of a benefits realization capability

1	A techno-centric mindset that placed the delivery of technical solutions at the heart of all discussions.
2	Lack of awareness that benefits-driven approaches were available.
3	Misconception that benefits were already being addressed (e.g. because a financial business case had been established).
4	Structural and cultural barriers to moving away from tried and tested systems development methods and approaches, resulting in lack of drive for change or failure of improvement efforts.
5	Structural and cultural barriers to changing the design of business processes and working practices, when implementing new software.
6	Inability to learn from previous experiences of poorly performing IT implementations.
7	Lack of leadership for development of the benefits realization capability.

study also provides important insights into why the establishment of a *benefits realization capability* has, thus far, been off the agenda for most organizations. These insights – which have been summarized in Table 8.1 – indicate that this is a multifaceted problem, but at its heart lie the twin problems of limited awareness of the possibility of different ways of working, and little appetite for moving away from their long-established systems development approaches.

Many organizations are in a 'mindset' where delivery of technology is seen as the objective of investments in IT and, as a result, there is no drive for the adoption of benefits-driven approaches. These organizations tend to adopt 'supply-side' solutions to the issues they see in realizing value from IT – these include off shoring and outsourcing. From a benefits perspective this is tackling the wrong problem. The 'benefits realization capability' is 'hidden in plain view' (Flynn, Wu and Melnyck, 2010) and is not a focus for management.

Building the benefits realization capability

Of all the organizations that I studied, only one had explicitly recognized that the only way in which they might regularly leverage significant benefits from their IT investments was by radically changing the way in which they conceived, conducted and managed IT projects. The way that this organization – a UK-based, governmental agency – achieved this *paradigm shift* in their approach to IT projects was through the establishment of a benefits realization capability, which had the following distinctive features.

Change the mindset

The first step in the establishment of the benefits realization capability was to break free from the techno-centric mindset, and to radically reposition the way in which IT is perceived within the organization: IT is now viewed as an *enabler of change, which has the potential to deliver benefits*, rather than being seen as a desirable and valuable resource, in its own right. Consequently, information technology is no longer viewed as the focal point and ultimate deliverable from software development projects, but rather as a potentially important ingredient in business transformation projects, which have far wider terms of reference. Whilst such a step might be easy to conceive, it is much more difficult to implement, as it requires a very significant and radical shift in organizational thinking and culture.

Adopt an explicit benefits focus

The point of departure for any business transformation project is to determine the benefits required by different stakeholders, and then to analyse what the organization will need to do differently, in order to deliver those benefits. Only when the required benefits, and accompanying organizational changes, have been specified, will the question of how information technologies might support or facilitate the specified organizational change can be considered. However, when evaluating different technical solutions, the capabilities of the software should not be ignored, and any potential to leverage the additional benefits or adopt more effective forms of organizational change should be exploited.

Strong emphasis on benefits planning and exploitation

Although the case organization had not developed a benefits realization capability that was explicitly composed of the same four components as our proposed model, there were many distinct similarities. At the initial project planning stage, there was a very clear focus on benefits for customers, other stakeholders and the organization. These benefits became the core focus of the detailed project planning and there was then an ongoing commitment to realizing these benefits through proactive organizational change, and the ongoing critical review of all project outcomes. Stakeholders were also empowered to take responsibility for the management of their own software, which ensured the ongoing exploitation of benefits.

Management of a portfolio of projects

A senior management team was responsible for benefits realization from the overall portfolio of projects and project managers were encouraged to look beyond the boundaries of their own projects, as benefits tend to arise from an integrated portfolio of projects, rather than from individual projects. Such an approach also ensured that lessons were learned and shared among project teams.

Proactive organizational redesign

The critical difference to traditional forms of systems development lay in the proactive approach to organizational redesign. For large-scale projects, this would be accomplished in the form of a formal business process re-engineering initiative, incorporating the critical review and explicit redesign of all constituent tasks, prior to the selection of the technology. Throughout the re-engineering initiative, the project team would frequently revisit the specified project benefits to ensure that they retained their position as the primary focal point of the project. The ultimate goal of the exercise was to guarantee that by the time that the chosen technology was ready for implementation, all the component tasks were clearly specified, all the accompanying job descriptions rewritten, and every effected member of staff thoroughly trained, and ready to play their part in the successful enactment of the new processes.

Adoption of a toolkit approach

The case organization was keen to move away from the use of traditional software methodologies to the use of a flexible 'toolkit' of practices, which could be tailored to the needs of specific projects. Many of these 'tools' are familiar elements of systems development, such as risk management, lessons learned, project boards, stage-end reviews, whilst others, particularly relating to organizational change and communication, were tailor-made. However, in all cases, the tools were applied with a clear and explicit focus on benefits realization. This approach was extremely powerful; it enabled business staff to get more effectively engaged in projects, as they were not working to complex project management and systems development methods. It also helped shift the focus from compliance with a methodology, to enabling teams to work successfully towards benefits realization.

Stakeholder-centric focus

The case organization no longer primarily viewed IT as a mechanism for the automation of internal processes and the replacement of people with technology. As noted earlier, their focus was on the realization of benefits, but it was particularly interested in delivering benefits that were important to internal stakeholders, and perhaps more critically, to the external recipients of its services.

Training and education

The governmental agency was building a shared understanding of the benefits-driven change process through providing education to all levels of managers to develop a common understanding of key elements of their approach to projects. The education was backed up by the role of the leaders of the transformation programme who, through their involvement in planning and controlling the projects, helped in establishing a consistent approach. The overall aim was to equip people with the knowledge and skills to work more effectively and flexibly, rather than ensuring that they complied with the dictates of a specific methodology.

Succeeding in breaking out of the techno-centric mindset

The experiences of the case organization show that it is possible to break free from the techno-centric ways of thinking, in which many other enterprises appear to be stuck. Essentially, they did this by recognizing that the development of the benefits realization capability was itself a strategic change programme. They applied the same principles and practices to this change programme as they subsequently applied to the realization of benefits from individual investments in IT.

The starting point was to put in place a leader, at the head of a core team, charged with radically changing the way in which IT projects were organized and managed, through the establishment of a benefits realization capability within the organization. A key role of the core team was to provide coaching, support and advice to help others involved in the programme to learn and develop, so that they could apply their knowledge flexibly to the needs of a specific project. A key element of the change programme to build the benefits realization capability was the establishment of a shared vision of the role and importance of benefits realization: a broad education programme to introduce some basic practices for benefits realization and to help employees apply them effectively supported this. Finally, a key element of the organization's success lay in establishing an organizational culture that encouraged and rewarded reflection and learning. This emphasis on learning was not only vital in development of the benefits realization capability, but also for the ongoing realization of benefits from individual projects. Consequently, there was a clear synergy between the management of the individual change programmes and the development of the benefits realization capability.

Opportunities for action: towards improved benefits realization from IT

The cost of failed IT projects across the globe runs into billions of dollars annually. The cost of missed opportunities is probably a great deal more. Consequently, in seeking to explore how more systems development projects might result in the delivery of benefits, rather than end in failure, this study has tackled a major issue. The most important contribution is to report on one company that has effectively adopted a proactive approach to benefits realization, and in so doing, has demonstrated that the key ingredient of its success is organizational change.

Organizations wishing to manage benefits more effectively must break out of their techno-centric mindset and adopt a benefits-driven approach to organizational change for their investments in IT and for developing the benefits realization capability of the organization. Action is required at a range of levels within the organization: individual projects and programmes of change; the overall portfolio of investments in IT and change; the wider competences of the organization for benefits realization including factors such as roles, skills, culture, performance measures and relationships.

Each organization will need to determine a relevant starting point and adapt benefits-driven practices to their specific needs and

Table 8.2 Important elements of a change programme to develop the benefits realization capability

Area	Action
Leadership	Leadership (and ownership) for the development of the benefits realization capability is important. *It will be important to identify a credible leader and leadership group, who can provide the vision and guidance for the development of enhanced competences.*
Education	Education and a framework for learning and ongoing support will be required to enable people to use the new practices effectively as they engage in benefits realization projects. *Education will be required for a wide range of individuals who participle in and lead benefits realization projects.*
Phased development	The capability will be developed through a phased programme of organizational change. The programme will evolve as changes to the organization enable learning and open up possibilities for further changes. *The leadership team will need to assess the current situation and guide the development of enhanced competences through a long-term change programme.*

current capabilities (Flyn, Wu and Melnyck, 2010). A benefits-driven approach can be adopted on a pilot IT project. Benefits reviews of completed projects would also provide valuable learning. At a portfolio level, the benefits-driven approach might help to provide a clearer view of priorities and to reshape the IT strategy. At an organizational level, there may be a wide range of issues to consider including IT governance frameworks, individual and departmental performance frameworks and role definitions and career development paths. Table 8.2 outlines important elements of a programme to develop the benefits realization capability.

Looking more broadly, there are also wider implications for management education and government policy to improve benefits realization from IT and to improve economic performance.

9
Big Picture

In previous chapters I have discussed the original development of the model of competences for benefits realization and a number of research projects that have explored aspects of the model. In this chapter I provide an outline of the model from the perspective of working with it in research, teaching and consultancy over a number of years. My aim is to bring the competences to life so that readers are able to make use of the model to help assess a situation and to make a difference.

Context – competitive advantage from IT

Ward and Peppard (2002) provided key starting points for the development of the model of competences for benefits realization. Benefits Management (Ward and Daniels, 2006) sets out a 'process of organizing and managing such that the potential benefits of IT are realized'. They propose a fourth era of IT based on the concept of an IS capability being the enabler of competitive advantage from IT. The focus on organizational competences that contribute to benefits realization and competitive advantage from IT has been widely adopted.

The perspective of organizational competences is powerful because it provides an insight into the complexity of organizations and does not prescribe specific process or structures, recognizing that key factors can be hard to identify. This is also its weakness. It can be hard to use it to develop practical guidance for individuals and teams in organizations, who are working to make improvements.

> *Box 9.1*   The toolkit of practices for benefits realization
>
> Following the initial work reported in Ashurst et al. (2008) we developed a *toolkit* of practices for benefits realization. It contained each of the practices written up in the form of a 'pattern' (Alexander et al., 1977, Coplien and Harrison, 2005, Manns and Rising, 2005) to provide a way of sharing knowledge related to benefits realization. This toolkit has gradually evolved based on further research and use in teaching.

The model of benefits realization competences is deliberately kept simple so that it can quickly be explained and used to help explore issues and opportunities in a specific organization. The toolkit of practices for benefits realization is designed to help in establishing the competences while leaving space for each organization to build on its strengths and focus as required on specific changes (Box 9.1).

In this chapter, the focus is on the model of competences for benefits realization. First, I consider the model in relation to specific investments in IT-enabled change. Then, I consider the implications for managing the overall portfolio of investments. As a third stage, the relationship with the wider organizational context is also explored.

Project perspective

The project perspective was a key starting point for the design of the competences model. The practices identified in Ashurst et al. (2008) demonstrate this as they are largely at the project level. The project perspective remains a valuable use of the model.

There is a broad similarity between the competences model and a project or investment lifecycle, which is useful. It is important to remember that these competences (each competence is defined as 'the ability of the organization to (for example) analyze stakeholder expectation') are not just stages in a lifecycle. Activities related to the different competences are likely to be taking place in parallel through much of the life of a project and investment. For example, Benefits Planning should continue through the life of a project to maintain a focus on benefits as new information becomes available and new opportunities are identified. Benefits Exploitation is important from the beginning of a project as planning for sustaining and developing benefits after 'going live' and completion of the original project is likely to be an important factor in successful benefits realization.

Benefits Planning

Benefits Planning takes an idea for a project and develops a clear understanding of the potential benefits for relevant stakeholders and the organization. It also involves exploring how the benefits can be realized. The benefits realization plan is one way to bring together the understanding of *what* the benefits are, and the plan for *how* they will be achieved.

Benefits Planning goes beyond the delivery of a business case, which all too often addresses the *what* and not the *how*. Business cases are often of limited value for benefits realization because they are written to gain approval of funding for the project, not to contribute to the actual realization of benefits. The gap can be surprisingly large; for example, a business case might put a financial value on time saved across a large number of people from introducing a new e-procurement system. That says nothing about if the benefits can actually be realized by reducing headcount or in other ways.

Benefits Planning is, or should be, an ongoing activity through the project. In a straightforward situation, reviews at key milestones will help to ensure that a project remains on track to deliver the intended benefits. In many other situations, where there is a greater element of innovation, there will be a need to revisit benefits planning at each stage. The understanding of the problem and/or opportunity will have evolved and there will be fresh insights into the potential benefits and how to realize them.

Benefits Planning is also the best place to stop bad projects if the benefits are not clear; the costs of realizing them are too high; or the sponsorship for the required business changes is not in evidence. There is a clear link to the portfolio perspective. If bad ideas don't get translated into failing projects resources can be focused on projects with the potential for adding greater value.

A number of well-established practices underpin the competence for Benefits Planning. It is vital to use relevant practices to bring together the high-level vision and the detailed planning for benefits realization, as well as liking to the design for the IT solution and the organizational changes.

Benefits Delivery

Benefits delivery takes the benefits realization plan and addresses the delivery of the IT solution and organizational changes required to achieve the potential benefits. It includes virtually all aspects of the 'IT project' that delivers the technology solution, related training, support materials and the support infrastructure. The IT project is now only one strand of a wider change project.

The toolkit for benefits delivery is also well established, and it draws on much of what we know about project management. Two of the most challenging areas are adapting the approach to a specific scenario and achieving the desired outcomes from the business changes.

Individuals involved in a project will adapt the approach they take based on the context and their experience. This is often fairly informal, and there are opportunities for many organizations to evolve this adaptation so that it is less adhoc and dependent on the individuals who happen to be involved. The IT and change portfolio can be used to help to think through how to adapt the approach to a specific project and can be a source of guidance for the senior management team responsible for the 'IT portfolio'.

IT has evolved from automating transaction processing (payroll, financial transaction and accounting) to a much wider range of scenarios which involve communication and collaboration between individuals and where the technology is used to informate rather than automate. In these cases, often involving professional or knowledge workers, the end user often has a lot of discretion about how (or if) they use the technology and the information provided through the systems. This brings a number of challenges, not least that designing and managing change becomes extremely hard. It is important to look beyond changes to business processes, particularly where these are about transactions, to a wider view of what is being changed: working practices, performance measures, skills, behaviours and so on. Models such as the 'cultural web and '7-S' are relevant. The link between cause and effect also becomes less certain.

Benefits Review

Benefits Review includes a number of different activities. One starting point is to reinvent the traditional post-implementation review to address benefits realization and lessons learned. The review explores the benefits realized (planned and unplanned); the reasons for changes from the plan; and opportunities for further benefits. The lessons learned element of the review considers what worked well and what did not in terms of the practices that contributed to benefits realization. The review effectively reflects on the *what* and the *how* of the benefits realization plan. Lessons learned need to be addressed in later stages of the current project (programme) and other projects in the organization as relevant. However, there is real risk of confusion here as the competence and the practice are both referred to as 'benefits review.' For the moment, I do not see a way out of this conundrum and hope that it is clear from the context which is intended. I normally refer to 'a benefits review' for the practice and to 'Benefits Review' as the competence.

Benefits Review is not just a one-off activity. Within the wider competence are two other major elements. First, the initial review prior to project kick-off, often referred to as an investment appraisal. I consider investment appraisal further as part of the portfolio perspective on the competences. Secondly, ongoing review during the lifetime of the project and investment.

Benefits Review can be considered as an ongoing activity during a project or the lifetime of an investment. There is certainly a need for focus at key project milestones:

- Is the project still on track to deliver the intended benefits?
- Have new opportunities for benefits been identified?
- Does the latest information on costs and the feasibility of the changes required to realize the benefits affect the project?
- Is the project still a priority for use of resources given the *current* level of knowledge and latest strategic context?

Benefits Review is a great example of the 'knowing–doing' gap. I suspect virtually every project method has some form of a post-implementation or benefits review and every project manager knows its importance. Yet, reviews are only carried out in around 25 per cent of cases. The goal is not to reinvent a post-implementation review as a benefits review. What is important is to get benefits reviews to happen consistently and to get benefits from carrying them out.

Benefits Exploitation

Benefits Exploitation goes beyond the end point of a project into service management (where ITIL is the dominant framework). IT investments often have long lifetimes, even in these times of rapid change and innovation. Core business systems can easily be 10–20 years old and even relatively fast-moving technologies such as word processors and intranet software can often be five years old. Benefits Exploitation includes sustaining business changes and ensuring continued benefits realization over the lifetime of these investments. This can include provision of training to help maintain knowledge as staff leave the organization, new staff join and others change roles. It also includes adapting to changes in customer needs and business priorities over these long periods of time. Crucially, Benefits Exploitation also reflects that these are often 'intellectual technologies' that have properties that are not fixed on implementation but can be innovated endlessly, depending on the interaction with the intellect of the human beings who implement and use them. As I learn more, I start to see new possibilities and become equipped for a further cycle of learning.

In most organizations Benefits Exploitation is neglected. IT effort goes into maintenance and keeping the systems running smoothly, but between the business areas and IT there is not enough focus on continued benefits realization.

Practices in the area of Benefits Realization are not well established. My toolkit of practices for benefits realization has some initial ideas. Exploratory work on knowledge worker productivity has highlighted the importance of this area and indicated opportunities for organizations to take action.

Building benefits competences at a project level

There are a number of possible starting points for developing competences for benefits realization (Box 9.2 provides some examples).

It is often valuable to start with Benefits Review. There will always be projects that have just completed or are in progress that would benefit from input in this area. An initial review can often be based around a two–three-hour workshop so the effort required is small. Reviews of a number of projects should add value to the projects themselves and enable realization of further benefits if the project itself is complete. The reviews will also provide insights into common

Box 9.2 Project-level starting points for developing benefits realization competences

Benefits Review (i)
Carry out a benefits review of a small number of recently completed projects.
Benefits Review (ii)
Carry out a benefits review of a small number of ongoing projects.
Benefits Planning
Pilot a benefits planning process on two–three projects.

issues and opportunities, and provide a starting point for planning wider action.

Portfolio perspective

We saw the portfolio perspective as an important part of the value of the model of benefits competences from the beginning. Subsequent experience supports this view. For an organization seeking to improve benefits realization from IT action at both project and portfolio levels is almost certain to be required. Recent work (Chapter 7) has started to extend the toolkit of practices for benefits realization to the portfolio level.

It is important to note that in many organizations the situation will be complex, partly, due to the lack of a common language. In a recent workshop an IT director referred to a 'project' that had been running for six years. In this case, the 'project' included an operational (live/production) service and probably a 'programme' (i.e. a series of projects all contributing to a strategic goal). In other situations, adoption of agile approaches involving rapid and incremental delivery of benefit from a series of releases, with planning taking place across multiple releases, blurs the boundary between a project and a programme. I would take a pragmatic approach, starting with current usage in the organization and aim to move to distinguish between project, programme and (operational) service.

The scope of the 'portfolio' varies in other ways. For example, does it relate to all projects funded from the IT budget or owned by the IT department? Alternatively, perhaps it looks more broadly at all projects which are affected by IT. There is also the time dimension: ideas for projects, live projects, completed projects and operational systems or services. Again, I would take a pragmatic approach and make a start with the portfolio at level that adds value in the short term. This might be a review of live projects or work on strategy that brings together ideas and priorities for future projects. A more comprehensive approach to managing the IT investment portfolio can then be developed over time.

A further important element to the scope of adoption of the portfolio is the organizational dimension. In virtually every medium or large organization, the portfolio will be valuable at a number of organizational levels (team, department, business unit etc.). The focus is on benefits from IT-enabled change. It does not matter if the IT function (infrastructure and application development) is centralized or local, even with a highly centralized IT infrastructure there is a need for a local business perspective on the portfolio. For example, the local portfolio needs to address the local implications of centrally driven projects, as there will be resource implications and presumably a need for local ownership of benefits realization. The local portfolio should also address local projects. There will usually be a range of important projects that can drive benefits realization that do not require central IT resource. For example, improved use of information or taking advantage of existing system features to improve efficiency or customer service (Benefits Exploitation). The portfolio has the nature of a 'fractal'; it can be usefully applied at any part of the organization.

This perspective also makes clear the organization-wide nature of the benefits realization capability. There is value in adopting key practices very broadly.

Benefits Planning

At the portfolio level the focus of Benefits Planning shifts to identifying which investments to make and to getting an effective overall spread of investments. The emphasis is on strategy and governance, in the sense of how decisions are taken across an organization by different individuals and business units.

The competence is particularly challenging. It requires good engagement across organizational units, professional disciplines and different levels of the hierarchy. There will be many challenges including politics. There are also inherent uncertainties that must be taken into consideration in some way: how is the business context going to change during the lifetime of this investment? How will new technology innovations create opportunities and when is the right time to make investments? These problems do not have a 'solution', but a number of practices can help to tackle these complex, problematic situations.

One response is to adopt some of the project-level practices at a portfolio level. For example, the tools of 'driver analysis' (Ward and Peppard, 2002) can be applied to the strategic question of 'where should I invest in IT-enabled change?' as well as to the project-level questions which include 'how does this planned investment contribute to the strategic objectives of the organization?' Equally, the 'benefits dependency network' (Ward and Daniel, 2006) can be applied at a strategy level, in which case the 'business changes' will represent programmes or strategic initiatives.

An architecture perspective is also valuable. This tackles the potentially adverse impact of a benefits-driven view of each project in isolation and looks across both the IT infrastructure and business organization (including business processes) to look at the big picture. Weill and Ross (2009) explore how to establish a 'digital platform' of coherent systems that allows accelerated innovation and benefits realization.

It is also important to adopt an agile perspective at a portfolio level to manage risk: speed of delivery and maintaining flexibility. A key agile principle is rapid, incremental delivery which means that the portfolio will give priority to short projects delivering benefits over a series of 'releases' of an IT and business solution.

Benefits delivery

Benefits delivery is about maintaining control of the overall portfolio to ensure benefits realization. At the portfolio level, important issues will include risk management, dependencies across projects, managing resource allocation across projects and exploring the business change impact of planned and current projects. Many issues become visible which will not be clear at an individual project level.

Issues of governance become important, that is which individuals and groups manage the portfolio. Weill and Ross (2009) are helpful here as well, providing a framework for IT governance. It is important to note that getting formal structures in place is only one factor. How people engage and behave is more important, because, ultimately, individuals and their relationships will determine effective governance.

At a portfolio level, many issues related to people become a priority. For example, what is the capacity for IT-enabled change and how can the capacity be developed in the short, medium and longer term? Who are the best people for a specific project? How can the available resources and the demand for investment be matched up across the organization?

The portfolio perspective also relates to management of IT applications and infrastructure. The IT and change portfolio implies that different approaches can be adopted to technology and service management depending on where an application sits in the portfolio. For example, an 'Exploratory' development might depend on pre-release software to gain insights from new technology and working with a strategic supplier. It is unlikely that the same approach will be taken for systems for Core Operations.

Benefits Exploitation

At the portfolio level Benefits Exploitation links strongly with service management. There is, however, an important change in perspective. The focus is continuing to realize benefits rather than simply to manage an operational IT service.

Staff turnover with time, the changing business context and ongoing learning about the potential of the technology are just three reasons why a continued focus on Benefits Exploitation is required.

Usually, too much is left to chance. Organizations should focus more on Benefits Exploitation. The returns from management attention are likely to be good. In most cases incremental investment will be £zero or £small and there will be valuable returns.

Benefits Review

Benefits Review is as critical at the portfolio level as at the project level. Investment appraisal is one area to focus on. Criteria for deciding when to invest in a specific project, to compare projects and to explore the overall level and balance of investment are hard to determine. Specifically, I note that traditional, financial driven models (payback, net present value etc.) are not a good fit for Strategic and Exploratory projects. This does not mean that rigorous assessment should be scrapped, but it would be helpful to have more appropriate criteria to help in making these key decisions. Traditional methods favour projects with a direct and easy to measure financial return, rather than projects that provide value to customers and contribute to strategic objectives. As a result, there is over-investment in 'Support' projects.

The benefits review concept is also critical at the portfolio level. Here a key emphasis is on making sure that effective reviews take place and that lessons learned are shared between project teams. The reviews need to take place for individual projects and then as a part of Benefits Exploitation reviews around live systems and business processes. There are significant challenges to enable both individuals and the organization as a whole to learn. It is important that the reviews do not become bureaucracy, but that they are used drive learning and increasingly effective management of the portfolio.

It is usually helpful to extend benefits reviews to a periodic review of the portfolio itself and related portfolio management practices. Review at this level can help reassess priorities and realign resources.

Building benefits competences at a portfolio level

It is inherent in the thinking behind the benefits competence model that developing the required competences is a complex and often challenging process of organizational change. The steps that are feasible and that will provide benefits will vary from organization to organization depending on a range of factors.

There are strong indications that the practices for benefits realization are very similar across different organizations. As a result, there is a considerable opportunity for organizations to learn from each other and to share practices. The challenge is then embedding adoption of new practices, and developing expertise in applying them, within a change programme that will be successful within a specific organization.

The research outlined in Chapter 6 provides indications of different levels of maturity in relation to different aspects of the competences. Developing to higher maturity levels can be related to adoption of further practices as well as more effective adoption of current practices. We are exploring if similar patterns of development can be found in different organizations. As a working assumption, we are using the idea of different 'playbooks' as a way to capture the development steps, or approach to a change programme, that can apply to a range of organizations.

There are a number of pieces of the jigsaw that contribute to competence development:

• The benefits competence framework at project and portfolio levels.
• The evolving toolkit of practices.
• An initial capability assessment designed to identify the current situation and priorities for change.
• Experience of working with one organization over more than two years as work to build competences for benefits realization.

A priority is to explore if different *playbooks* can be established to provide guidance for organizations on how to approach competence development and the first steps to take.

It is vital to keep the focus on organizational change, not on IT implementation. But here, as in other areas, IT can be an important enabler of change. Combinations of portfolio management software and Web 2.0 approaches enabling collaboration and knowledge sharing can help to develop competences for benefits realization at a number of levels. They can provide a clear framework for project and portfolio management, improving efficiency and effectiveness. For example, a clear project lifecycle can be established and used consistently with agreed templates for key deliverables. It can enable collaborative working at a project level and can facilitate effective management for the portfolio by providing increased visibility of key project information; for example, 'traffic light' reporting of project status and progress against key milestones. Key benefits tools can be supported, for example, by consistent ways of capturing key information, for example, from a stakeholder analysis. Approached in the right way, the technology can enable creative and flexible working by saving time on areas that don't add much value, by enabling collaborative working and improving communication. The Web 2.0 emphasis can also be valuable in enabling organizational learning and knowledge sharing. For example, collaboration around specific tools can be valuable and can help individuals and teams to apply them effectively.

The ideal situation is to embed adoption of IT support into a wider programme of change to develop the enhanced competences for benefits realization.

Organizational perspective

The organizational context is an important influence on benefits realization. Recent work by Brynjolfsson and Saunders (2009), drawing on a whole series of earlier studies, provides strong evidence of a number of organizational level factors that contribute to benefits realization. This perspective is a valuable addition to my findings at project and portfolio levels.

Bringing the viewpoints together suggests that in the right context there can be broader benefits from individual investments in IT. For example, Microsoft made a major push to get rid of paper forms and succeeded. At one level this would be a series of Support investments with relatively limited payback. Overall, however, it provided a strategic initiative to push the boundaries of what was possible and to find out how to resolve problems, such as meeting legislative requirements, and handling the need for signatures. The learning could be shared with customers and there were wider benefits in terms of the agile, low bureaucracy work environment that contributed to priorities, such as attracting and keeping talent and being a great place to work.

From my earliest work on benefits realization I have identified a range of factors at an organizational level. These include (but are not limited to):

- The role of the CIO including his/her relationship with other senior leaders and the leadership they provide for developing a benefits focus.
- The general organizational culture and climate and the extent to which learning is possible. For example, one case study provided an example of an organization where it was very difficult to say that some thing had gone wrong or that improvements were needed so that it was very difficult to learn and improve.
- The impact of HR policies and practices. For example, the role of project managers and how performance is defined; if there is a

development path that encourages 'high flyers' to get involved in leading change projects and the extent of cross-organizational working.

A number of these factors are discussed in the study reported in Chapter 5.

Learning organization

Building the organizational capability for benefits realization can be considered as *organizational learning*. Two different perspectives help us in understanding how to share learning and put it into practice. In an article and book about the Learning Organization, David Garvin (1993, 2000) refers to three overlapping stages of organizational learning:

- Cognitive: members of the organization are exposed to new ideas, to expand their knowledge and begin to think differently.
- Behavioural: employees begin to internalize new insights and alter behaviour.
- Performance improvement: changes in behaviour lead to measurable performance improvement.

We need learning at all three stages. Garvin defines a Learning Organization as 'an organization skilled at creating, acquiring, interpreting, transferring and retaining knowledge and at purposefully modifying its behavior to reflect new knowledge and insights' (Garvin, 2000). This is an important element of our overall benefits realization capability – specifically to purposefully modify behaviour. He goes on to identify a number of enablers of learning:

- Create the opportunity to learn from all experiences – both good and bad – admit to failures.
- Foster an environment that is conducive to learning – make time to really understand customer needs, to think and reflect.
- Open up boundaries and stimulate the exchange of ideas.
- Create learning forums – reviews of strategy or cross-functional processes, including internal benchmarking.

A second perspective on learning is provided by Pfeffer and Sutton (1999) who refer to the gap between what we know and what we do. This 'knowing–doing' gap is a serious issue in the arena of IT-enabled change, as many valuable and widely known practices are not effectively adopted. The lack of adoption of the practice of carrying out a post-implementation review (benefits review) is just one of many examples.

Box 9.3   Approaches to sharing learning

Updating policy and evolving the project framework (i.e. making change in the formal organization).

- Introduce a specific project lifecycle framework.
- Focus project board activity on milestone reviews.
- Capturing and sharing reusable resources.
- A communications strategy (or other deliverables relating to the approach to the project) may be highly reusable.
- Capturing aspects of tacit knowledge.
- A project team has a 'brown bag' session (open workshop over lunch) to share their experience in a specific area.
- The team writes a short case study/prepares a podcast.
- Learning is captured as a new 'practice' to add to the toolkit.

Sharing knowledge through people

- Key players from the project are moved into other teams specifically with the goal of sharing their experience of new ways of working.

Training and education

- Standard courses are updated to reflect learning.
- A course provided to introduce an agile, benefits-driven approach to projects.
- Education is provided in specific areas identified as gaps and high priority.

Experiments

- An agile approach is piloted on an Exploratory project using an external coach to support the new way of working.

Reward and recognition

- The CIO uses regular departmental briefings to recognize innovators.

Using networks

- Staff are encouraged to participate in external professional networks and attend conferences – with an emphasis on bringing back ideas to share with colleagues.

Pfeffer and Sutton suggest that a major reason for the gap is that education and development focus on 'know-what' (to do) rather than 'know-why' (the underlying principles) and 'know-how' (the skills built up from experience of putting the knowledge into practice).

It is clear that although we can have valuable benefits review sessions the results will be limited if we do not take purposeful action to follow them up. Learning can be shared in a number of ways and this has to be planned and managed (Box 9.3).

Summary

In this chapter I have provided an outline of the model of competences for benefits realization, considering project, portfolio and organizational perspectives. I have also considered aspects of the wider organizational context that relate to the competences. Insight into the competences is a starting point for making use of the model to help to assess a situation and to make a difference. The 'learning organization' provides insights into the development of these competences.

In the next chapter I consider the relationship of practices to the competences for benefits realization. The final chapters then explore the development of the competences and areas for further research.

10
Practices and the Development of Competences for Benefits Realization

There are a number of further implications of the work to date for the development of organizational competences for benefits realization. This chapter explores how the idea of 'practices' can be used in practice. It then goes on to explore further factors related to practices, and how they can contribute to the development of competences for benefits realization. First, the importance of clear 'principles for benefits realization' that provide the basis for a benefits mindset or paradigm and help guide the selection of relevant practices. Secondly, the value of the format provide by the idea of 'patterns' as a way of capturing and sharing what works. Patterns are presented in the context of key challenges identified in the knowledge management literature. Thirdly, the need for a common project framework within which the practices can be enacted. Finally the importance of effectiveness, it is how the practices are enacted that is important. Practices are envisaged as a resource to equip teams involved in IT-enabled change, not a new form of 'methodology'.

Practices in practice

The cases explored in previous chapters raise a number of issues about how to apply the concept of practices. These issues are explored in this chapter. First, the granularity of a practice and how to match the granularity to the context is considered. The cases provided evidence of practices at a number of different levels of granularity that contributed to the successful outcome of projects. Secondly, the shift from a practice focused on solution delivery to one focused on benefits realization is explored. There were indications that a range of practices contributing to an agile approach to solution delivery could, with a change of perspective (paradigm), become practices for benefits realization.

Below I explore risk management as an example of a practice and illustrate how a practice can be applied to IT solution delivery or benefits realization with relatively small changes. Granularity of practices is explored by considering if this is one practice or a number of different practices.

An example: risk management

I *could* look at risk management as a success factor for IS projects. I am *not* taking this perspective. I consider risk management as one of a number of practices that contribute to competences for realizing benefits from investments in IT. The emphasis on *how* to ensure risk management contributes effectively to success in benefits realization.

The mind map for benefits-driven risk management (Figure 10.1) is based on a simple risk-management process and shows important success factors for risk management (Microsoft Solutions Framework: Risk Management Discipline v1.1 White Paper – June 2002).

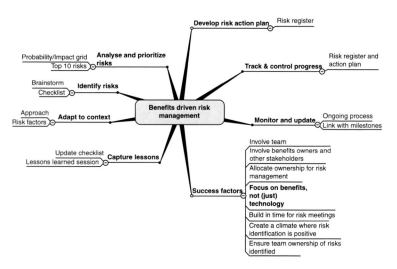

Figure 10.1   Exploring risk management as a practice at different levels of granularity

Granularity

In the framework of practices developed in this research, risk management is a practice (BP10/BD6 – see Appendix 2). At a more detailed level risk management could be seen as comprising a range of practices for *identifying* risks, *capturing* lessons and so on. I think that it would be reasonable to call them practices as they have a specific output and meet the definition of a practice. The mind map covers the overall practice and the different branches are broadly related to the more granular practices.

There is probably a connection between the appropriate level to describe, share and use practices and the experience of the people involved. For relative novices a more detailed level, giving more guidance, is relevant. For experts a higher level is relevant; the details they will decide for themselves. In a way, I think this fits with Checkland's description of different ways that SSM is used (Checkland and Scholes, 1999). The mind map helps to encourage thinking in this way – with different levels of detail. The more granular set of practices may also be relevant if there is a specific problem with how risk management is carried out in a particular context.

Perspectives on a practice – solution delivery vs benefits realization

The cases from the knowledge base studied in Phase 1 (Chapter 4) adopted a consistent approach to risk management. They followed the Microsoft Solutions Framework, which is also reflected in the mind map. These projects were successful in delivering solutions. The City Council studied in Phase 2 (Chapter 5) used PRINCE2 as the core of its approach and emphasized the importance of risk management. In this case, the focus of the projects was on specific benefits.

In these different cases, the core of the risk management activity was very similar. The difference was in how the goals of the project were defined: the focus was on solution delivery or benefits realization. Risk management as a practice is essentially the same – the difference is the *goal it is applied to.*

This strong similarity of the core practice for solutions delivery and benefits realization applies to a range of other practices. Particularly in Phase 1, where an agile approach was adopted with a focus on involving people and effective teamwork, a number of practices related to solution delivery would, with a change of objective, become practices that contribute to benefits realization. This suggests that, for some situations, the critical factor for adoption of benefits-driven approaches is a change of perspective to focus explicitly on benefits as a goal and that if this can happen, actual day-to-day practice does not need to change significantly. Existing skills are relevant with a change of paradigm or mindset.

Principles for benefits realization: a new mindset and the basis for a 'common language'

One of the facilitators of benefits realization identified in the research is a 'consistent framework and common language'. This is closely linked with how practices contribute to the development of competences. The original model of practices developed as a starting point for this research (Chapter 4) was based on the general *principles* of a focus on benefits from people doing things differently (Ward et al., 1996). Schultze and Boland (2000) suggest that practices are related to general principles that provide a context for the description of *what* is to be done. These principles represent 'know-why', which Pfeffer and Sutton (1999) stress is critical in bridging the 'knowing–doing' gap and gaining adoption of new ways of working. They stress that 'know-what' and 'know-how' are not enough. The model of the development of competences addresses the importance of 'know-why' (Ward and Peppard, 2002). The resources that contribute to practices include attitudes and behaviours, which they link with 'know-why'.

The work by Ward and others on Benefits Management (e.g. Ward and Daniel, 2006) highlights some key principles that underpin the approach. A similar approach to making key principles explicit is also seen in practitioner work (Highsmith, 2004). The evidence from this research suggests that these principles, representing 'know-why', are an important factor in organizational competences for benefits realization. They provide part of a common language and set of attitudes.

There are good precedents in both academic and practitioner literature for this approach. Examples include:

- Principles for benefits management (Ward and Peppard, 2002).
- Principles for socio-technical design (Clegg, 2000).

- Propositions for the socio-technical design of information technology systems. (Eason, 1989: chapter 4).
- Principles for agile project management (Highsmith, 2004) and the agile manifesto (www.agilemanifesto.org).
- Principle for DSDM (Dynamic Systems Development Method – www.dsdm.org).
- Principles for the Microsoft Solutions Framework (an approach to solution development and project management).

The benefits management principles set out by Ward and Peppard (2002) provide a focus on realizing value and have been used as a starting point for a set of principles for benefits realization. By themselves, they are insufficient, as they do not address *how* people work together to realize benefits. In building on this foundation a key step was to consider the scope of the four competences already outlined and the role of *people* in the successful realization of benefits, particularly the project team and issues of wider stakeholder management. Principles addressing these broader factors draw on work by Eason, Clegg and the 'agile' software development movement.

The set of principles (Box 10.1) is a starting point, and there is an expectation that they will evolve over time as the emphasis and

---

Box 10.1 Succeeding with investments in IT – principles for a benefits-driven approach

1. Performance only improves when people do things differently.
2. Motivated individuals and teams, with the environment and leadership they need, will deliver innovation and value.
3. Focus on the delivery of value to customers and other stakeholders throughout the lifecycle.
4. Realization of benefits will depend on the participation of all relevant stakeholders.
5. Benefits arise when new capabilities are exploited and managed to the advantage of stakeholders.
6. Exploitation of the potential of IT requires a major form of an organizational and individual learning.

Note: The principles draw on work by the Agile Alliance, Chris Clegg, Ken Eason, David Preedy and the Microsoft Solutions Framework team, and John Ward.

detail of the wording is refined. Together, the principles represent a worldview (Checkland and Scholes, 1999). The principles provide a foundation for the specific benefits-related practices. Different principles would result in different practices, for example, with a focus on technology delivery or less of a focus on people and stakeholders.

Adoption of benefits-focused approaches to IT is a 'paradigm shift' (Johnson, 1992) in perspective. Making this shift is potentially a significant challenge for individuals and organizations. The different paradigms can be characterized by adherence to different principles. A difference in paradigm was seen in Phase 1 where solution delivery was taken as a measure of success by most organizations (see Chapter 8). This reinforces the importance of 'know-why', the principles that underpin the adoption and use of specific practices. This is an important subject for further research – how individuals and organizations can be enabled to make that shift.

Patterns as a way of capturing and sharing practices: knowledge management and organizational learning

Practices and patterns

Practice is an increasingly widely used term, and a range of descriptions and definitions have inevitably emerged. Wenger et al. suggests the following definition: 'a set of socially defined ways of doing things in a specific domain: a set of common approaches and shared standards that create a basis for action, problem solving, performance and accountability'.

Not only does the concept of a practice appear to be very closely aligned with how people actually work, it is also particularly relevant in knowledge-intensive activities, such as IT projects, where much of the effort is based upon the experiences of individual and teams. Moreover, the concept of practice relates to the informal organization and how work is *actually* done by individuals and groups.

For my purposes, I have made the following distinctions:

- A *practice* relates to an approach to getting work done in a specific context. Some authors refer to practices as 'routines.' Practices are what people *do* within your organization.

- A *pattern* is an abstraction, a description of a practice. It must lose some of the richness and uniqueness of the related practice but it provides a way to identify and communicate what works. I have used the concept of patterns as a basis for the benefits-driven toolkit for IT-enabled change.

The format of a 'pattern' provides a valuable way to capture and share practices for benefits realization.

Patterns as a contribution to knowledge management

An important strand of thinking about knowledge management is the distinction between explicit and tacit knowledge. This categorization of knowledge as either explicit or tacit is likely to be misleading: there are different levels of tacit knowledge and of skills. In some cases, important aspects of tacit knowledge can be made explicit while retaining much of its value. For example, some 'tacit skills could be articulated readily if organizational members were simply asked the question 'how do you do that' (Ambrosini and Bowman, 2001)?

Thompson and Walsham (2004) showed that if knowledge is to remain useful once made explicit, a link with the *context* in which the knowledge was used and so in which it might be reused must be retained. They also noted that while the ideal of 'strictly explicit knowledge is self contradictory', there are still opportunities to codify some aspects of knowledge that will be useful, particularly with a specific context as provided by, for example, a community of practice. Kamoche et al. (2003) use the jazz metaphor of improvisation in suggesting that there is an 'optimal amount of structure'.

The jazz analogy is that skilled professionals, whether jazz musicians or people engaged in a multidisciplinary team to deliver IT-enabled change, need some common understanding to work together. This is not a score to follow note by note, but a common language; common ways of working provided, for example, by the benefits principles and toolkit.

The tension between codifying nothing, thereby risking the loss of important information, and trying to codify everything, risking banality, is at the very core of attempts at knowledge management.

The codification of practice into knowledge is of its essence an active and social task 'connecting people so that they can think together' (Alvesson and Karreman, 2001), bringing together different people with different experience and enabling them to contribute their knowledge in a team (Becker, 2001). The goal is to enable group learning by the 'sharing of individual interpretations to develop a common understanding' (Bontis et al., 2002).

Alexander, Ishikawa and Silverstein (1977) produced a book of design patterns, so named after the pattern books of architectural scholars, furniture makers and others, which were the means of disseminating good practice from the time of ancient Rome. Their 253 patterns covered topics ranging from regional planning to interior design. Each pattern is a brief description (usually a page or two) of a problem setting out how the problem arises and issues relevant to its resolution. It leads to a recommended action or solution. A pattern is a way of sharing advice based on experience of what works in similar situations. The format of a pattern, with an explicit focus on the *context* in which it is useful and explanation of the *forces* impacting a situation, makes it particularly suitable for many areas of project management, which are complex and require judgment based on experience. The pattern helps to make explicit and communicate important elements of what would otherwise remain tacit.

The pattern also includes reference to other patterns, either because they contain information, which may be needed fully to understand the recommended course of action, or because that action might affect them. In this way, the patterns form a network of linked patterns – the Pattern Language (PL) – in which each pattern is small enough to be comprehensible while the connections provide the richness necessary for using the patterns to tackle real world problems.

From usage in object-oriented software engineering, the pattern language movement within the software community has grown to include more work on software architecture (Coplien and Harrison, 2005), interface design (Borchers, 2001) and other issues. Wider uses of patterns are also emerging, for example, in providing guidance on how to introduce new ideas into an organization (Manns and Rising, 2005). In education too, the use of patterns, particularly as they might enhance eLearning, is a growing area of activity. Patterns provide a valuable way of capturing and sharing good practice and contribute to the development of the benefits realization capability of an organization.

In summary: the format provided by a pattern provides a powerful way of capturing and sharing knowledge in complex, knowledge-intensive environments where it is impossible to make key aspects of knowledge fully explicit. This is the foundation for the approach of capturing and sharing practices for benefits realization.

Practices provide a basis for a shared language and a way of working that enables business and IT leaders, and multidisciplinary teams engaged in realizing benefits from IT-enabled change, to work together effectively. In practice, individuals, teams and organizations will build expertise in using the tools and learn to adapt them as they apply them in a range of situations.

Example of a pattern

The example 'round tables' (Box 10.2) shows how the 'patterns' can be documented. It comes from guidelines we developed with participants at a series of workshops.

Box 10.2   A simple example of the patterns format for capturing and sharing knowledge

Round tables

Forum meetings are held at round tables to encourage discussion.
We want to develop an atmosphere of learning from each other. This means that the speakers must not dominate the sessions and that there must be opportunities for interaction in small groups and across all the attendees.

* * *

Traditional programmes tend to line up their students in large tiered lecture theatres so that they can focus on the speakers. By contrast, in the Forum we will restrict numbers in order to maximize debate.

We will be seated café-style, at round tables in order to enable engagement in immediate and deep discussion whenever an opportunity presents itself. This layout encourages fast and efficient interaction to take place within and across table groups.

* * *

The round tables, by themselves are not sufficient to ensure that we have participative sessions. We will also rely on the **50:50 rule, learning by doing** and the **variety of meetings** to encourage discussion, debate and learning from each other.

The structure provides a link with the specific context(s) in which the knowledge is useful. In addition to the 'solution' (recommendation for action to improve the problematic situation), a rationale is provided to give insight into the complexities of the situation and the reasons the solution works. *Rationale* and *context* are vital so that users have the understanding to adapt and improvise as they apply the knowledge in their situation.

In the *round tables* example, we adopted the following structure:

- **Name**: the name seeks to capture the essence of the pattern.
- **Summary** (often with picture): the summary supports the name and reinforces the understanding of the pattern.
- **Context**: a brief statement that indicates the context and relevance of the pattern.
- **Rationale**: it explains the different forces involved in the problematic situation and how the solution responds to these forces. In these examples, this section is kept brief. The proposed **solution** is in bold.
- **Links:** these are given to related patterns.

The example in Box 10.2 is very brief. A typical example is 2–3 pages. A number of slightly different formats are used for patterns.

Common project framework

A clear and consistent project framework was identified as an important facilitator of benefits realization in a number of projects. Ward and Peppard (2002: p. 610) explore the role of a 'process' in providing a link between resources and competences. They describe a process as a set of activities, with an emphasis on flexibility and people collaborating to achieve a particular goal. Practices provide a flexible way for people to work together to establish competences as part of a flexible 'process' – in the context of an investment in IT the 'process' can be referred to as a project *framework*. The City Council (Chapter 5) used PRINCE2 as the basis of a common framework. At another case-study organization, a significant issue was that there was no common framework shared by the different stakeholders involved.

Develop craft skills to enable benefits realization

A key lesson is that benefits realization depends on the *quality* of enactment of the practices and not simply which practices are adopted. This in turn depends on the knowledge, skills (know-what/ know-how) and the 'know-why' (Pfeffer and Sutton, 1999) of a focus on benefits realization.

The skilled professionals engaged in projects are not followers of rigid methods but highly motivated 'craftsmen' (Sennett, 2009), passionate about the job, and skilled in using a range of tools, which they can adapt, based on experience to the specific situation they are facing. Sharing and adopting practices provides a way to improved performance.

Building competences through organizational learning

As adoption of benefits approaches, that is the development of competences for benefits realization, is an organizational change, there are likely to be big hurdles to be overcome by organizations if they are to succeed. One potential outcome of attempts at improvement, observed in the research, is that benefits approaches are enforced, but in practice are subverted and simply become a focus on financial targets with no real impact on project activities or the mindset of those involved.

Evidence so far suggests that the development of competences will need to be seen as a strategic initiative that may involve substantial change and will take place over a period of time. Gradual adoption of practices for benefits realization with an emphasis on building skills and effective enactment of the practices is an important element of the change programme. A common language (provided by clear principles for benefits realization) and a common project framework are also important. The perspective of organizational learning provides useful insights into the change programme to develop competences.

11
Making a Difference – First Steps in a Change Programme

The chapter draws on an ongoing action research programme, which is seeking to develop the benefits realization capability of a large organization (a Russell Group University). The chapter will outline the approach and the initial results to provide some starting points for other organizations.

Introduction

Exploitation of Information Technology (IT) is a priority issue for the Higher Education (HE) sector. As Sir Ron Cooke noted in his contribution on behalf of JISC (www.jisc.ac.uk) to the debate on the future of HE, 'UK higher education enjoys a world-class ICT infrastructure; this should be maintained. But more effective *leadership*, at all levels, is required to exploit this infrastructure.' This view is consistent with the report by the British Computer Society and the Royal Academy of Engineering (2004) suggesting that the success rate of IT projects in the UK is only 16 per cent and reported estimates of wastage due to IT project failures as $140 billion in Europe. Higher Education is a particularly challenging area for benefits realization from IT for a range of reasons, including the federal nature of HE institutions (HEI) and the importance of non-financial benefits, such as improvements to research quality or the student experience. The general economic climate and the specific pressure on HE funding only increase the importance of exploiting existing assets and getting value from new investments.

The project is seeking to gain insights into how organizations can develop the competences required to succeed in realizing the potential of investments in IT to deliver benefits to stakeholders and improve organizational performance. In contrast with prior work, the project (1) focused on the development of organizational competences for benefits realization rather than the adoption of a specific method; (2) involved participatory action research to explore how the competences required for benefits realization can be developed; (3) examined what is required to help organizations to develop the required competences themselves.

Organizational competences for benefits realization are considered at three levels. First, the practices adopted on specific projects and the success of the projects in benefits realization. Secondly, the management of the entire portfolio of IS projects, including deciding which projects to invest in; sharing learning from project to project; and resource planning and development. Finally, both projects and the overall portfolio will be considered in the overall organizational context: for example, the impact of organizational structures, performance measures, management education and career development. Opportunities for intervention at all three levels are being considered as part of the action research programme.

In outline, the stages of the project are as follows.

Phase 1: engage – preliminary activity

This preliminary stage involved assessment of the current level of competences for benefits realization and consideration of priorities for improvement. A preliminary view of benefits and measures of success for the project was also established and refined as part of the development and approval of the proposal for funding.

The initial assessment that there was a strong foundation of integrated systems and a sound IT infrastructure was supported by further experience during this period. Table 11.1 sets out specific opportunities for improvement identified during this period, and how they relate to the project.

Table 11.1   Initial view of challenges affecting benefits realization

	Challenge	Approach in this project
1	Project process and adherence to good practices.	A separate project is seeking to establish more consistent approaches to projects across the university.
		As part of engagement with the five pilot IT projects, there will be some opportunities to explore wider aspects of project practice.
		At a later stage in this project, I will address incorporation of specific benefits practices into the overall project framework.
2	Setting priorities and taking into account learning.	Priority setting is one aspect of management of the overall IT portfolio that will be considered as part of one of the Exploratory projects.
3	Post-implementation reviews.	Reviews have taken place successfully on a number of projects, but the practice has not been consistently applied, and the related feedback loop established. This is incorporated within the 'benefits review' workshop, which forms a core part of the 'toolkit'.
4	Having a 'seat at the table'.	Specific challenges include:
		• the need for the capacity to engage at top level, given that – 'IT is related to virtually every strategic issue.'
		• the ability to communicate/deal with unfashionable issues at senior management level (security, etc.).
		Relationship building is a key element of the Benefits Workshop programme.
5	Exploitation.	Exploitation of existing systems, services and information is addressed by one of the Exploratory projects.
6	Delivery capacity.	Change delivery capacity (i.e. how the existing resources can be used most effectively to tackle IT-enabled change) is addressed indirectly through the Benefits Workshops.
		More importantly, work on setting priorities (as part of the Exploratory project on portfolio management) will help to make the most of the available capacity.

Phase 2: explore – initial assessment and building engagement

The priority at this stage was to extend the core team to the senior IT management team as a whole. A workshop was held with the IT senior management team as a first activity to broaden engagement in the project. This session explored the opportunities and challenges of benefits realization from IT. It resulted in good support for the assumption underpinning the project proposal; that it was a good time to shift focus from technology delivery to benefits realization. The discussion also provided useful insights into challenges and opportunities that will be valuable as the project progresses.

A further workshop session was held at the suggestion of one of the IT management team members to explore 'what does success look like' and to discuss the intended benefits of the project and how to achieve them. It was very valuable to share in this thinking as a team and to build on the work done on benefits for the proposal. As the work took place on IT strategy and planning it became increasingly clear that the adoption of a benefits-driven way of working was an important enabler of a range of strategic objectives. It was encouraging to note the adoption of a benefits-driven way of working has become a major priority for 2010–2011.

Table 11.2 Projects within the overall programme

Strand	Outline
Benefits Workshops	Five one-day workshops introducing key elements of the benefits toolkit and applying them to participants' projects. Also a major emphasis on development relationship and engagement skills.
Engagement with core IT projects	Project teams apply elements of the toolkit to five important projects from different areas of IT.
Exploratory projects	Projects exploring specific areas where good practice is not well established. Three areas are tackled: senior management engagement with IT (e.g. Huff et al., 2006); exploitation of existing systems and information; and benefits-driven management of the IT portfolio.

Phase 3: evolve – real time learning from applying benefits practices to key projects

This is the core of the project and involves a number of strands of activity (Table 11.2).

This phase of the work was also broken down into a number of 'versions', each with distinct deliverables. These versions became the focus for managing the project. Existing practices for a benefits-driven approach to projects (based, for example, on Peppard et al. (2007)) were brought into the research as a 'benefits toolkit'. This toolkit was a key element of the Benefits Workshops and the engagement with projects.

Core activities in Version 1 included running the first two Benefits Workshops; launching the external project website; launching an internal collaboration site for the project team and participants in the workshops; and an update and review session with the Registrar. During Version 1, the IT senior management team was also engaged in considerable work to plan and launch a new structure for the department. This will continue through Versions 2 and 3 as individuals take on new roles, and relevant moves take place to establish working spaces for new teams.

As a result of Version 1, approximately 30 people have been introduced to the benefits-driven approach and key elements of the benefits toolkit. They have also had opportunities to try out applying elements of the toolkit to the five pilot IT projects during the workshop sessions.

Phase 4: evaluate

Capturing of evidence, reflection, evaluation and learning are ongoing elements of the programme. For example, the discussions at every project meeting and workshop have been documented. Learning has been facilitated as part of core team meetings, meetings of the Steering Group and at the Benefits Workshops. This is an example of something which is good practice, and outlined as such in many methodologies, but is often not done: '90% of projects do not have a comprehensive post-implementation review.' The aim is to change the culture so that this type of reflection is simply designed into projects. The project framework adopted for the research provides excellent opportunities for periodic review and reflection.

This chapter is based on a paper produced by four of the project team members as part of ongoing reflection and review.

Looking ahead

The evolutionary approach being taken to the project is proving successful. The main objectives and main strands of activity are clear. Detailed plans will continue to be evolved version-by-version, as the project proceeds, enabling learning and innovation, as well as taking advantage of unexpected opportunities. At this early stage of the overall project, I feel that the learning to date in a number of areas is worth discussing further and communicating to a wider audience. I have considered (1) learning about IT projects and ways of working; (2) wider issues of building the benefits realization capability; and (3) learning about the approach to this research project. These learning points feed into further cycles of the action research.

Findings from engagement with IT projects

Pilot adoption of the benefits-led approach

Key members of each of the project teams attended the five one-day workshops run as part of the Benefits-led IT project. At each workshop, I introduced part of the benefits toolkit and participants had the opportunity to apply the ideas to their projects with input and feedback from their colleagues. At workshops 2 and 5, each project team provided an update on their project including progress, challenges and the contribution of the benefits toolkit. I also had feedback sessions with individuals to get their views on the benefits-led project and to explore their progress in adopting the toolkit. These sessions took place after workshops 2 and 4.

The initial projects were chosen to reflect different sizes and degrees of complexity, and different stages in the project lifestyle. Short case studies provide insights into the projects and the lessons learned from the work to adopt benefits-driven practices.

ReCap

The vision for the ReCap project was clear from the start: to enhance student learning, in particular, to provide a resource to help international students; to enable students to think about concepts during lectures without having to worry about taking notes; to support revision; and to enhance support for different learning styles. The system is now in place in 50 lecture theatres (Summer 2010) to provide automatic recording of lectures and is being widely adopted.

A Benefits Review session takes the form of a lively workshop exploring the actual benefits realized through a project, both expected and unexpected, along with project practices, assessing what worked and where improvements could be made. It's about taking time to reflect, learn and enable further benefits to be realized and further innovations to take place. I ran a Benefits Review session with the ReCap steering group and the learning was shared at workshop 5.

For ReCap, a key priority is to get more staff recording lectures and more students using the recordings. The main action is to market the existing capabilities to new users by sharing some of the staff and student stories of the benefits they have gained from the system. There is also work to do to emphasize the benefits to new groups of staff and students as the system is deployed to other departments. The team has also been aware of the need to avoid raising expectations too high, particularly prior to full university-wide deployment. I hope the pilot users will continue to provide ideas and encouragement to others as ReCap moves from an exploratory pilot to a university-wide capability.

What is clear from the feedback I've had is that ReCap provides a new capability for the university; the precise benefits will emerge only as people start to *use* the technology. The unexpected benefits come as staff and students start to use the technology to work in different ways. Also new ways of getting benefits are emerging as the users' experience and confidence develops. ReCap is now evolving into a programme of activity as the scope is extended to include desktop video capture, which will open up a wide range of new opportunities.

ReCap provides a good example of the importance of what we refer to as Benefits Exploitation. The quest to leverage benefits from software should not cease as soon as it has been implemented. Continued focus is required over the life of the investment. It also shows the importance of a wide range of stakeholders – benefits realization from IT is not just about management of the IT function. ReCap had strong academic leadership throughout, working very closely with IT and this was an important factor in the success to date.

The team found many aspects of the benefits toolkit helpful: the stakeholder analysis and focus on stakeholder engagement; consideration of non-financial benefits and the links of benefits with change. The project is a good example of the need for business leadership and a focus on benefits, in this case for staff and students. Following the Benefits Review session with the steering committee there is a sense that the project as a whole is thinking in benefits terms: adopting a benefits 'mindset'.

NESS

NESS has been developed outside IT, by a team in the Computer Science department. It has evolved into playing a key role in the student-assessment process across half the University, and it is gradually being integrated with other core systems. NESS supports marking assessment and exam-board activities: taking the marks from the academic markers through external examiners to final classification. Significant savings in effort and elapsed time have been realized in the Schools that have adopted the system (17 at the time of the review). In addition, there have been quality benefits, as the time saved allows more time for checking and reviewing, and because summarized and exception data (e.g. the spread of marks on a question or module) is available from the beginning of the process.

The NESS team adopted key aspects of the toolkit and developed a benefits realization plan and stakeholder analysis. They have found that the 'benefits approach is very clear' and that as a result 'people are thinking differently'. 'It's a very clear language that is helping communication with people and contributed to better working relationships' (NESS Project Manager).

Key learning points include the value of allowing opportunities to emerge. The success of the early stages of NESS has revealed significant unexpected benefits, which were then used as a basis for further developments. NESS also illustrates the need for management of change at a local level as more Schools have taken on the system – encouraged by the success of early adopters. For IT, a portfolio perspective is critical. NESS might have been seen as a maverick, but with communication and cooperation, it has been allowed to play an important role and is being integrated with wider systems.

P2P

Procure to Pay (P2P) is sponsored by the Finance Director of the University with the goals of achieving more effective procurement and more efficient processes. There are opportunities for significant cost savings from rationalizing spending across different suppliers and being able to take early payment discounts. The process will be more flexible for users offering a 'click to buy' purchasing experience and enabling better use of time.

The project is challenging as it affects the jobs of a large number of people across the university. During the benefits-led project, initial work on P2P included the formation of a steering group, a project team and progressed system selection.

The P2P team have adopted many of the benefits-led ideas and found the work on stakeholder mapping extremely valuable. This contributed to the overall project structure, for example, with clear roles for HR and the departments affected. In addition, there has been a major emphasis on communication with early union briefings and a 'road show' to affected departments. The team commented: *'change management tools can never be implemented too soon.'*

Key learning points from the project include the challenges of actually 'banking' benefits even in an apparently clear-cut situation. P2P will save a lot of time, but this will affect the jobs of many people. There will be a lot of work to establish how these time savings are translating into a range of benefits. The organization-wide impacts also require input from many areas to deliver (HR, Procurement, a joint IT/Finance project team, Schools and Departments). The benefits-led approach is helping these different groups work together to deliver the changes and there has been significant early effort to build stakeholder engagement. Success will depend on continued engagement and the willingness and ability of the different Schools and Departments to manage the changes locally in order to realize important aspects of the overall benefits.

NuMed

NuMed is a major University initiative to set up a medical school on a campus in Malaysia, in new buildings. It involves a range of stakeholders in both countries, for example the contractors responsible for the new building. The curriculum is directly linked to the well-established medical school. The IT element is a critical, but limited, part of the overall project. Teaching on the new campus will depend on getting the right IT capabilities in place and having good links with the existing school.

A number of learning points have emerged. First, the value of the stakeholder mapping exercise, which quickly revealed that action was required to draw together the different strands of activity (HR, Estates, IT, Medicine, UK, Malaysia) and establish more integrated programme management with sponsorship related to the overall benefits and strategic goals rather than specific components (the new campus). There is an opportunity for IT to take on a more general programme management role, which they tend to play by default, as they have an awareness of the issues and the skills required. NuMed also highlighted the importance of non-financial benefits. Although clearly strategic for the University, the direct financial impact is relatively small because of the financing arrangements, so the project has not triggered the enhanced focus reserved for 'large' projects. From a portfolio perspective, the project has absorbed considerable senior management time and highlights that this is a key issue in terms of capacity for change. The impact on a small number of senior individuals is often underestimated. The Benefits Review process has also helped to crystallize learning from NuMed, which is now being applied to another major international project.

Testing Disaster Recovery

The aim of the Testing Disaster Recovery project was to respond to Audit Committee and carry out a test of existing contingency arrangements. This was seen as the start for a longer-term programme of work to develop enhanced backup and recovery capabilities.

A key challenge for the project was to bring together different stakeholders and establish a shared understanding of the goals. Although apparently clear, it revealed, as with other projects, the major challenges of getting a good, shared understanding of the goals. The benefits approach plays an important role because of the emphasis on stakeholders working together in well-designed workshop sessions, which help to bring out into the open different assumptions and understandings. In this case, the tension was between carrying out a test that would prove the recovery capabilities (the requirement as perceived by the project manager) and carrying out a test in a reasonable timeframe and with limited resources as a first step (the requirement as perceived by Audit Committee members in the workshops).

Learning about IT projects and ways of working

A number of general learning points are based on the reflections of the project team from the benefits workshops and the engagement with the pilot projects.

Clarity of IT project objectives and scope

There seems to be some fuzziness about the goals of the various IT projects. For example, where a project includes the Estates department, Human Resources, IT and an academic department, do all the players have the same understanding of the vision, objectives and scope? Is there a governance structure to bring together all the different projects and activities contributing to the overall goal? It will be important to check out if this fuzziness is a communication issue or if the scope, objectives and/or roles are not clear at a detailed level. Is there an effective way of translating the senior management vision into appropriate programme objectives, roles and structures?

Common language and ways of working – project framework

A second aspect of fuzziness affecting the scope and objectives of the projects is an apparent lack of a common language or set of concepts. For example, some of the 'projects' seem to be tackling a programme of various individual projects as well as management of an ongoing service. The split between programme, project and service management is not clearly defined with relevant goals, roles, governance and so on. There would probably be considerable value in greater clarity.

Consulting and teamwork skills development

Although much of IT work is about projects, the participants in Benefits Workshops 1 and 2 apparently had limited experience of creative and collaborative approaches to team working. This seems an increasingly important element of the benefits toolkit and will be emphasized in later workshops. There also seem to be limited day-to-day opportunities for people to spend time working together outside their teams' silos, for example, to share learning. Is there a way that it can become business as usual to collaborate and share?

General learning points

A number of general points emerged from the work with the specific IT projects.

- First, the benefits-led approach resulted in a significant shift in thinking and focus. Stakeholder engagement and organizational change were emphasized. The benefits perspective brought people together and provided valuable insights into how different elements of the projects fitted together.
- The approach required, and encouraged, more collaborative working based on an understanding of the benefits and the cross-department team effort required to realize them. Perhaps more importantly in the longer term, the interactive approach helped in building relationships between people, teams and departments and encouraged people to have fun. This is a very promising start for an increasing focus on innovation enabled by IT.
- In many cases, there were important, unexpected benefits, which were a major driver of value in new phases of work.
- There was strong support for the Benefits Review activity – which provided space to think. The sessions were an important enabler of new insights and shared learning.
- In several cases benefits realization was an ongoing process of learning, as people worked with the systems and discovered opportunities. A key challenge, and opportunity, is to facilitate this learning across the organization, for example as individual lecturers or programme teams find ways to use ReCap to enhance student learning and experience.
- Finally, many of the projects, even an apparently transactional project such as P2P, required considerable learning and change at a local level in Schools and Departments. This highlights benefits realization as an organization-wide capability.

Developing the benefits realization capability of the organization

A number of broader learning points relate to the development of the benefits realization capability of the organization.

Skills to engage with and influence senior managers

Many of the issues of benefits realization come clear as I consider the big picture – what is the real scope of a project, how does it align with the University and IT strategies, how does the role of the sponsor align with the goals of the project? Many of these things are big issues and often are closely linked with people at one or more levels higher in the hierarchy than the people involved in the projects on a day-to-day basis. Individuals tend to tackle the job they have been given to do (scope and objectives) and do not have the time, access, confidence, communication skills and management support to explore or challenge the bigger picture. For example, if the scope of the project appears poorly defined, there are gaps in the governance framework and how it is working, then it may be vital to engage senior management and convince them to take action. There is a premium placed on courage and communication skills if some of the bigger issues are to be raised and tackled. There is also a need for senior management to listen and to create an environment that is open to reflection, learning and challenge.

Many of the challenges identified in the research relate to dealing with people – for example, communication with senior stakeholders, reflecting and learning lessons. It is vital to focus on these skills and how people go about project activities rather than just what process they follow and what tools they use.

Linkages with other initiatives

It will be interesting to see how progress on the project is affected by other activities – for example, the restructuring of the department. This must certainly have distracted the IT senior management team at a crucial stage after Workshop 2, when the priority was to follow through and relate the toolkit to the five major IT projects. Restructuring also provides an opportunity as it becomes clear that the benefits approach is a crucial enabler of a new way of working, allowing the restructured organization to work more effectively and, in particular, to engage with wider stakeholders in the university.

The complexity of the project

Since I wrote the initial proposal, the project has developed to be seen as a strategic initiative for IT with the goal of developing competences for benefits realization. Although this is very positive, it also brings into focus the complexity of the project and the linkages with other Strategic projects, particularly the restructuring of IT; staff development; introduction of relationship management roles; the evolving project management framework; and considerations of the role and scope of IT, for example, in response to changing expectations as 'digital natives' become students and staff.

The benefits-driven, evolutionary approach being taken to the research appears a good fit for this complex environment. It also suggests a comparison with the challenges of leadership in developing excellence in teaching, where the recent Leadership Foundation for Higher Education (LFHE) report suggested that at least five years is required to make a difference (Gibbs et al., 2009).

Capability development as a benefits-driven programme of change

The project has approached developing the benefits realization capability of the organization as a benefits-driven programme of change. The approach has emphasized key benefits practices: the active leadership of the IT Director; extensive engagement with the IT senior management team to build shared understanding of the goals and engagement in the project; and engagement with an initial core group of stakeholders from IT and other areas of the University. This focus on engagement has taken time and effort – but so far, it seems to have been valuable. The need for this focus on stakeholder engagement and participation will continue as the project reaches out more broadly in the organization.

The picture will become increasingly complex, as we need to build, maintain, and develop engagement, adoption, learning and feedback across different groups. There is a sense in which ideas 'cascade' from the IT senior management and core team, but equally important are the opportunities for feedback, learning and evolution as the ideas are put into practice and established as 'business as usual'.

Learning about the approach to the research

We also reflected on the approach taken to the research and highlighted a number of learning points.

Value of an agile approach to the research

The plan for this project has deliberately been left flexible and I have evolved the approach based on the various streams of project activity and a number of major 'versions'. This has allowed a number of innovations that were not explicit in the original plan: for example, the linkage of the initial benefits workshops into a five-day leadership programme and linkage of Exploratory project work with other partners (a regional IT Directors Forum). This agile approach has worked very well and has allowed us to remain broadly in line with the outline plan in the original proposal.

It has also been very encouraging to see participants bringing forward suggestions for aspects of the approach that had not yet been made explicit or discussed with participants. For example, the workshop with senior IT managers (4 December 2009) provided the suggestion that we must adopt a benefits-driven approach to adopting benefits-driven ways of working – which is, of course, a core principle, but had not been discussed at all at that stage. The suggestion resulted in a further session at which we discussed 'what does success looks like', along with the target benefits for the project. Participants in the first two benefits workshops also raised the need to get broader engagement from outside IT, which again was part of the longer-term plan but had not been discussed at that stage.

There is also some evidence here about the value of different approaches to communication, sharing of ideas and gaining engagement – for example, although the original proposal had been circulated to the IT senior management team, it was only through engagement in a series of workshops that understanding and engagement was built. This is a learning that we can take back to the five IT projects and is an area where we need to develop the benefits toolkit. It reinforces the major focus on communication and engagement that is required as part of any project or change programme.

Value of the toolkit and benefits workshop approach

The two initial Benefits Workshops were designed around the benefits of toolkit and the concept of a number of 'workshops', each of which demonstrated how the elements of the toolkit could be put into action on a project. We need to reflect on the design of the two days and the extent to which we have succeeded in presenting the ideas as workshops that the participants can take and apply (perhaps initially with some support) to their projects. We will continue to assess what resources are most valuable to the participants – both initially, and then over time, as they try to adopt (and adapt) the ideas on their own projects.

Experience so far suggests that there is a lot of value in the current workshop process where the ideas can be communicated person to person, and there is an immediate opportunity to try them out with colleagues, whilst working on real-world projects.

Value of the participant oriented action research

The participative action research approach has worked well and provided a bridge between participants and researchers, supporting the view (Lee, 1999a) that we are one community and that there is a linkage between the research process, skills and tools, and what it takes to be effective in practice. A challenge we need to explore further is getting feedback from participants alongside everything else that is going on. The key to doing this in a way that adds value to participants is the direct link with 'reflective practice' so it does not become an activity that is only of value to the external researchers.

Conclusions

The contribution of this project will be to provide new knowledge about how to tackle the 70–80 per cent failure rate of IT projects and reduce the wasted expenditure reported at around $140 billion per annum across Europe (BCS, 2004). This is a significant problem for organizations and although some previous research has explored this area, there has been limited impact on practice. The project is starting to produce resources aimed at practitioners to help organizations to develop the required capabilities for benefits realization. It will also provide the foundation for further research, based on the approach of Neely et al. (2000), that tests out the resources as part of a wider process to enable practitioners to take action to enhance competences for benefits realization with limited support. This would then provide the basis for much wider action to develop these important competences.

Conundrum

A key challenge is how to plan a benefits-driven approach to developing a benefits realization capability, when the plan has to be owned and led by the local team. Complications arise from the fact that the local team does not (yet) have a detailed understanding of the benefits approach and toolkit at the start of the project. There was certainly a shared view of the high-level vision, but not of any detailed aspects of the 'tools' and process involved. A key success factor is the strong relationship between the external advisors and the internal team. The iterative approach is also proving particularly valuable.

12
Reflections on Research Methods

I have kept the discussion of research methods very brief in earlier chapters and in this chapter reflect on the research approach and its evolution during the programme of work.

My aim is to try to share some lessons learned for others adopting a participative approach to case studies and action research. I draw in part on a recent conference paper where I explored the possibility of a more 'agile' approach to research.

Context

Transforming research into practice is a topic of great importance to me personally. I have spent 30 years in a variety of roles as a Chartered Accountant, IT manager, and Information Systems (IS) consultant and, most recently, as a teacher and researcher at a Business School. My main research focus is enabling organizations to develop the IS capability required to realize the potential of information systems (Peppard and Ward, 2004).

We know there is a major gap between theory and practice and many successful practices are not widely adopted (BCS, 2004). This 'knowing–doing gap' (Pfeffer and Sutton, 1999) is a crucial factor affecting my wider teaching and research. This is an important context because I am adopting an interpretive philosophy for this research, and, as a result, I have made clear something of my background and assumptions to enable the reader to evaluate the main discussion in this chapter. As Harvey and Myers (2002: p. 177) note: 'the researcher does not suspend their own prejudices – they become critically aware of them – making them explicit in the process of learning.' This is important as 'researchers' prior assumptions, beliefs, values and interests always intervene to shape their investigations', so you need this information to help assess this research (Orlikowski and Baroudi, 2002: p. 66).

From the beginning of my work on this research I saw it as an 'agile' project (Boehm and Turner, 2004; Highsmith, 2004) and as far as possible attempted to apply my experience as an IS professional and project leader. One implication was to see the research project as being delivered through a number of major phases marked by milestones at which progress was assessed. The approach was very much in line with the recommendation by Silverman (2000: p. 68), quoting Miles and Huberman, to 'begin with a foggy research question and then try to defog it'. Some of these phases are presented through the different chapters in this book.

The researcher enters the problem situation with a guiding framework of ideas and 'theories' (Checkland and Scholes, 1999). This then evolves as the research progresses. The initial proposal for this research was to use the concept of a 'learning organization' (Garvin, 1993, 2000) as a conceptual framework for exploring how an organization could develop a capability to realize benefits from IT. As a result of the literature review and initial engagement with the problem, I narrowed the focus to concentrate on exploring the competences and practices required for an organization to realize benefits.

Aim of the research

The research programme is seeking to build on a number of strands of previous IS research relating to, for example, socio-technical approaches to IS, benefits management, project-success factors, IT project evaluation. This work has provided valuable insights, but, as the continued high failure rate of IT projects suggests, has not yet succeeded in transforming practice. In particular, the research is exploring the value of practices and competences as ways to overcome the barriers to the adoption of benefits-driven approaches to IS and to enable organizations in developing the capability to realize benefits from IT.

In this chapter, I explore the overall research philosophy and strategy including considerations of validity and generalizability. Then I discuss specific research methods that have been applied, specifically case studies and action research. Finally, I explore the applicability of agile principles to relevant, participative research. *You will have to judge for yourself if you want to skip this more 'technical' chapter.*

Philosophy and strategy: the foundations for the research programme

The purpose of IT projects is considered to be delivering benefits to stakeholders (Jurison, 1996). Business changes enabled by IT are required in order to realize the benefits. As a result, it is important to consider IT in an organizational context and to consider the impact of the context on the projects (Markus, 2004). This approach, of considering the project in the organizational context in which it takes place, provides the opportunity (Silverman, 2000: p. 69) of 'using a zoom lens – zooming in and out to maintain perspective' and gains insights as the project and the impact of its context are considered.

Interpretive perspective

Considering the philosophical perspective is helpful to make more explicit some of the assumptions about 'what constitutes "valid" research and which research methods are appropriate' (Myers, 1997). Interpretive researchers 'start out with the assumption that access to reality is only through social constructions such as language, consciousness and shared meanings' (Myers, 1997). Interpretive studies attempt to understand phenomena through 'the meanings people assign to them' (Myers, 1997) and interpretive methods of research in IS are 'aimed at producing an understanding of the context of the information system and the process whereby the information system influences, and is influenced by the context' (Walsham, 1993: pp. 4–5).

Avison and Fitzgerald (2003) relate this to the systems paradigm and work by Checkland. In contrast with the scientific paradigm, which copes with complexity by reductionism, 'breaking things down into smaller and smaller bits for examination and explanation', they argue that a system has emergent properties (i.e. the whole is greater than the sum of the parts) and that therefore it is important to study the system. Studying only of the parts cannot provide an understanding of the system as a whole. Human activity systems (Checkland, 1981), which are the subject of information systems research, are systems, which do have emergent properties, and therefore from this perspective a reductionist approach is of limited value.

Checkland and Scholes (1999) argue that soft systems approaches are a better way of understanding the complex world of organizations than 'hard' structured analysis methods. They also contrast soft systems, which are a way of modeling and *thinking about* real-world activities to develop understanding, with the hard systems viewpoint that the real world being described is a system. This description helps to relate different IS methodologies to either a positivist or an interpretive perspective.

From an interpretive perspective, Lee (1999a) suggests that the distinctive element of social science research is that humanly created meanings are an integral part of what is studied. This means that research must address not only 'objective', observable behaviour, but also the meaning this behaviour has for the people involved. He suggests that this has no counterpart in the natural sciences, the foundation of a positivist perspective – where atoms do not attach their own meaning to the world around them. Lee also explores the role of the researcher from an interpretive perspective. The researcher is not an independent, detached observer. The researcher becomes a 'human instrument of observation' and the research depends on their ability to understand and respond (1999a: p. 17).

Hermeneutic foundations

Hermeneutics refers to both a philosophical foundation for interpretive research (Myers, 1997) and a range of research methods that originally referred to reading ancient texts (Lee, 1999a). Lee suggests hermeneutics is a valuable method as it helps to relate the specific words or human behaviour to the context – either the passage and text as a whole or the organizational and social context. Lee (p. 20) relates the idea of the 'hermeneutical circle' to understanding human behaviour: 'I would come to an understanding of a single action by relating it to the whole organizational setting: and reciprocally, I would come to understand the whole of the organizational setting by relating it to individual actions.' This approach is relevant and is adopted at a range of levels within this research as, for example, projects are considered within their organizational context.

Lee (1994) quotes Ricouer (1981) and Taylor (1976) to argue that the hermeneutic approach is valuable for studying 'individuals their actions and organizations': 'Many scholars have extended their conception of text to include not just the documentary artifacts that human subjects create but also their individual actions, group behaviours and even social interactions, all of which as *text analogues* have meanings that can be read and interpreted.' Myers (1994) also supports the value of a critical hermeneutic approach, which brings together critical and interpretive perspectives. Myers refers to Gadamer (1976: p. 117) to identify the hermeneutic circle, the analysis of the parts in the context of the wider whole, and the overall situation in the context of the individual situations as a key aspect of the approach. This fits well with the scope of this study as the research design explicitly considers the projects as part of the wider organizational context and change capability. Boland (2002: p. 229) also refers to Ricouer (1981) to support treating the 'situation as text' so that actions and situations are also understood as text.

Participatory paradigm

Breu and Peppard (2003) make the case for a *participatory paradigm* for IS research where researchers conduct an *inquiry from the inside* together with the research subjects. A driver for this work is to respond to the rigour vs relevance debate and the need for practical relevance of IS research. In this context, they point to limitations in both positivism and interpretivism as both these philosophies have emphasized the researcher as a detached observer and aimed to reduce subjectivism. They seek to build on the tradition of interventionist research, for example action research (Checkland, 1981) and by integrating reflection and action, theory and practice, to produce knowledge with greater potential for practical relevance (Breu and Peppard, 2003).

Breu and Peppard (2003) outline support for a participatory paradigm. They stress that it is essential to assess the value of research using criteria that are based on the paradigm. For example, it is not appropriate to use criteria that are drawn from a positivist paradigm to assess interpretive or participative research. Referring to Rowan (1981), they suggest that the level of involvement of the research subjects in participatory research can vary significantly from that of subjects in action research, to full collaborating partners in participatory enquiry. They outline a set of principles that together outline a participatory research philosophy (paradigm) (cf Avison and Fitzgerald, 2003: p. 557). This includes a *political* principle (Breu and Peppard, 2003) that implies a change in the role of the researcher and that they *engage* together with the practitioner in the knowledge creation process. In line with the *practical* principle (Breu and Peppard, 2003) there is an awareness that the researcher 'changes the system and social world of those being researched' through the entire research process. This is in line with other forms of qualitative enquiry. From a participative perspective this impact is recognized, and seen as important, but the researcher does seek to 'avoid imposition' during the research. The *epistemological* principle provides a theory of validation through which the outcomes from research can be judged. Breu and Peppard (2003) suggest that validation of the knowledge occurs through several mechanisms and they specifically refer to co-creation and co-implementation of models from the research.

The goal of participatory research is practical or 'useful' knowledge (Worren et al., 2002). They suggest this practical knowledge has a different form from 'scientific' knowledge and that it is in concrete, everyday language and that it is necessarily ambiguous, yet 'it can draw on a common vocabulary and frame of reference among those participating in its creation and use' (Breu and Peppard, 2003: p. 189). This common vocabulary is important throughout the research process. This useful knowledge emerges from an interaction between conceptual understanding and practical application and needs to be judged by the extent to which the actions and tools generated in the research process produce the intended goals and are adopted by the practitioner community.

The participatory paradigm links well with the fourth dimension of MIS that is put forward by Lee (1999a: p. 9) 'no MIS researcher is, or even should be, an objective, disinterested scientist. MIS researchers seek to *contribute* to the documentation, innovation, or illumination of better ways in which people in organizational contexts use, manage and maintain information technology…. MIS researchers *want* Hawthorne effects – we want our observations and theories to make a difference'. He suggests that (some of) the subjects

(IT workers/professionals) of MIS research consider themselves a profession and that MIS researchers are part of that profession and to an extent are responsible to and must serve the profession. The role of the researcher is not that of an observer but as a *member* of the professional community with the subjects of the research. This links well with the work by Schon (1983) on improving professional practice.

Peppard and Breu (2003) do not put forward an ontological principle, but building on the work by Lee (1999a) and Schon (1983) it is appropriate that participatory research is about *becoming*. The participative researcher, as a member of the professional community is *becoming* more effective as a (reflective) practitioner. The practitioner, as a member of the participative enquiry is also *becoming* a researcher, a more effective practitioner, and this could also perhaps be described as becoming a reflective practitioner (Lee, 1999).

Research strategy

An interpretative and participative foundation for the research has been established. This approach is well aligned with the overall goal of the research which is to produce 'relevant and timely' research (Davenport and Markus, 1999: p. 20) and to 'produce knowledge about how to intervene in the world and change it in order to satisfy real-world needs' (Lee, 1999b: p. 29). It also fits the area being addressed by the research which resembles the situation described by Lee (1999b: p. 32) 'the practitioner's organizational environment is murky, and the variables are not even known' rather than the situation put forward by Benbasat and Zmud (1999) where the researcher tests and validates a theory specifying dependent and independent variables and the relationships between them.

The research strategy must be matched to the research context. Lee (1999a) identifies a number of dimensions of Management Information Systems (MIS) that influence the value of different research strategies. First, Lee (1999a: p. 7) suggests that 'MIS involves not just information technology but also its instantiation': 'There are rich organizational and political processes whereby a set of information technology is instantiated and there are also rich organizational and political processes pertaining to the continual managing, maintaining and changing of the information technology instantiation' (Ibid.). Secondly, he suggests, 'MIS involves, as reactive and inextricable elements, both an information system and its organizational context.' Lee suggests that an 'information system and its organizational context each have transformational effects on the other'. He refers to work by Markus and Robey (1988) that suggests that there are emergent properties of information systems, as also described by Checkland (1981). This is also in line with a socio-technical perspective, which implies that the focus should be on the system as a whole, not on the separate social and technical systems alone. As a result, 'the information system and the organizational context must be studied, understood and managed together, not separately' (Lee, 1999a: p. 8). Thirdly, Lee (1999a) suggests, 'MIS involves information technology as a form of *intellectual* technology.' Information technology is an intellectual technology not an industrial technology in that it has properties that are not fixed on implementation but can be 'innovated endlessly, depending on its interaction with the intellect of the human beings who implement and use it' (Lee, 1999a: p. 8). This can lead to an ongoing cycle of innovation and change as the technology extends the intellects of its users leading to further innovation.

These factors underpin the approach taken to this research. In particular the projects and information systems that result from them are considered in their organizational contexts and the completion of software development is not seen as the end point, but just another milestone in an ongoing activity to realize benefits.

A key challenge in the area covered by the research is the gap between theory and practice and the lack of widespread adoption of benefits realization methods. The research is exploring whether this lack of adoption is due, at least in part, to not taking into account sufficiently the complex nature of organizations. Qualitative techniques will be used to investigate these complex problems, as 'the beauty of qualitative research is that its rich data can offer the opportunity to change the focus as the ongoing analysis suggests. Such changes of direction reflect the subtle interplay of theory, concepts and data' (Silverman, 2000: p. 63). Specifically the research programme has included case studies and action research.

Validity and generalizability

The validity of research should be assessed in the terms of the paradigm on which it is based. Breu and Peppard (2003) do not develop specific guidelines for assessing participative research, so the principles for conducting and evaluating *interpretive* field studies in information systems proposed by Klein and Myers (1999) are taken as a starting point for exploring principles relevant to this research, which is adopting a participative emphasis to an underlying interpretive philosophy. Klein and Myers (1999) suggest it is important for researchers to decide which of the principles are relevant to a particular project.

Given the interpretive/participative perspective of this research, the researcher is not an independent, detached observer. The researcher becomes a 'human instrument of observation and the research depends on their ability to understand and respond' (Lee, 1999a: p. 17). The researcher will 'naturally form an understanding with the help of a pre-existing understanding that I carry with me' (Lee, 1999a: p. 20). This pre-existing understanding is part of what it means for the researcher to be part of the same professional community with the other participants of the research, which allows effective communication and understanding. It is an important contributor to the outcomes from the research (Miles and Huberman, 1994: p. 38)

Classic criteria for research quality are internal validity and external validity. Internal validity is 'generally defined as the trustworthiness of inferences drawn from data' (Herr and Anderson, 2005: 50). Lincoln and Guba (1985) are referred to as a basis for taking 'trustworthiness' as the extent to which the researcher's interpretations are credible, or 'ring true' to those who provided the data. External validity refers to 'how well these inferences generalize to a larger population or are transferable to other contexts' (Herr and Anderson, 2005: p. 50).

Herr and Anderson (2005: pp. 54–57 (and in various papers)) set out five proposed validity criteria for action research:

1. *Outcome validity*: did actions occur and did they lead to resolution of the problem that led to the study?
2. *Process validity*: to what extent are problems framed and solved in a manner that permits ongoing learning of the individual and/or system? This includes what counts as evidence and the quality of the relationships that are developed with participants.
3. *Democratic validity*: is the research done in collaboration with all parties who have a stake in the problem under investigation? If

not done collaboratively, how are multiple perspectives taken into account and how is the 'relevance' of the findings to the problem determined?

4. *Catalytic validity*: to what extent does the research process reorient, focus, and energize researchers and participants to a deeper understanding of social reality and action to change it?

5. *Dialogic validity*: is provided by a form of peer review. For example, this might involve the inclusion of a 'critical friend' in the research process who can help in exploring alternative explanations of the data. Similarly, there may be a role for a more formal review group.

There are various other sources on quality criteria for action research. Lau (1999) provides an analysis of some of these. Eden and Huxham (1996) provide a further set of criteria in a general-management journal. They refer to the *outcomes* from action research and the *process* of action research. They emphasize theory as both an input and an output, and the need for structure in the research and the process of exploration of data.

Herr and Anderson (2005: pp. 61–64) provide an interesting discussion of generalizability (external validity). They draw on work by Lincoln and Guba (1985: p. 298) to make a distinction between generalizability and *transferability*:

> If there is to be transferability, the burden of proof lies less with the original investigator than with the person seeking to make the application elsewhere. The original enquirer cannot know the sites to which transferability might be sought, but the appliers can and do. The best advice to give to anyone seeking to make a transfer is to accumulate empirical evidence about contextual similarity; the responsibility of the original investigator ends in providing sufficient descriptive data to make similarity judgments possible.

They also refer to work by Stake (1986) who in turn draws on work by Polanyi (1958) and Schon (1983) to argue that practice is often guided less by formal knowledge than by knowledge based on personal and vicarious experience. Stake refers to the value of a 'naturalistic research report' in which the reader gets a sense of the individuals and the unique situation. Readers recognize similarities with situations of their own and may be stimulated to think about their situation in new ways. This perspective fits with practitioner culture where 'stories are shared daily among practitioners as part of an oral craft tradition' (Herr and Anderson, 2005: p. 63). Given the gap between academic theory and workplace practice, that is the lack of adoption of academic theories and guidance, it may be very helpful to think more about how to transfer and how to communicate the results of research in different ways, for example through stores and examples. The concept of patterns (Jessop, 2004) might also provide a way to communicate aspects of research findings, for example, as they provide a clear link with the context in which the knowledge is applicable.

Walsham (1993: p. 15) notes that 'the validity of an extrapolation from an individual case or cases depends not on the representativeness of such cases in a statistical sense, but on the plausibility and cogency of the logical reasoning used in describing the results from the cases, and in drawing conclusions from them'. On this basis, the final judgment must remain with the reader.

Case studies

As Yin (1994: p. xv) states the case study may be the most appropriate research method for appreciating the complexity of organizational phenomena. Yin (1994: p. 13) describes the characteristics of the case study as a research strategy. 'A case study is an empirical enquiry that investigates a contemporary phenomenon within its real life context, especially when the boundaries between phenomenon and context are not clearly evident. The case study enquiry copes with the technically distinctive situation in which there will be many more variables of interest than data points, and as one result relies on multiple sources of evidence, with data needing to converge in a triangulating fashion, and as another result benefits from the prior development of theoretical propositions to guide data collection and analysis.'

The case study is appropriate 'when "how" or "why" questions are being asked, the investigator has *little control over events* and when the focus is on contemporary phenomena within some real-life context' (Yin, 1994: p. 1). The case study can be used for exploratory, descriptive or explanatory purposes – depending on how the strategy is applied and what type of questions are being asked. Case studies can be positivist (Yin, 1994), interpretive (Walsham, 1993) or indeed critical.

One factor underlying the problems with adoption of benefits-related methods is potentially a 'paradigm filter' (Johnson, 1992). If this is the case, a paradigm shift is required to see the problems from another perspective and to make a breakthrough in gaining adoption. Remenyi et al. (1998) suggest that the case study enables narrative thinking – 'a consistent story that describes the essential features of the problem under consideration'; this is 'essential in facilitating a shift between paradigms'. This reinforces the value of the case-study approach for this research project.

As a result of these factors, the case study was adopted as the research strategy for this project. The following section explores how the case-study method was used to align with the research philosophy.

As Silverman suggests, 'theory development as part of the design phase is essential' (Silverman, 2000: p. 27). From a different perspective, Checkland and Holwell (1998) stress the importance of making explicit the framework of ideas and methodology before entering the real-world problem situation. This research has been approached in a number of phases, to allow theory development to occur, and to allow learning through a number of cycles of research and reflection.

I entered the empirical phase of the work having established a framework of competences and practices for benefits realization as described in Chapter 3. However, as Eisenhardt (1989: p. 536) states, it was recognized that the research constructs were tentative at this stage. The aim was not to verify and validate the framework of practices in a 'positivist' sense but to explore its usefulness in understanding and explaining the situation, and in the longer term of being useful to practitioners. In particular, the in-depth study of a successful organization presented in Chapter 5 aims to follow Dyer and Wilkins (1991: p. 617) and provide a good story that is an 'exemplar of a new paradigm' rather than to focus on confirmation of the individual practices in the proposed framework. This use of a specific and detailed framework in the context of interpretive and hermeneutic research follows Davis et al. (1992), one of the good examples of interpretive case studies recommended by Myers (1997).

Throughout the analysis, 'theory is used as a sensitizing device to view the world in a certain way' (Klein and Myers, 1999: p. 75). There was an 'iterative process of data collection and analysis, with initial theories being expanded, revised or abandoned altogether. A simple metaphor for this latter case is the use of scaffolding in putting up a building, where the scaffolding is removed once it has served its purpose' (Walsham, 2002: p. 105). In this research the practices framework was used as an initial guide to design and data collection, as part of an iterative process of data collection and analysis, and was a final product of the research.

Conceptual maps were used to try to provide a clearer view of the 'complex conceptual structures' emerging from the 'thick description' provided by the case write-ups (Walsham, 2002). In addition, memos/vignettes (Miles and Huberman, 1994) were used to explore a number of key themes and attempt to gain deeper insight into the complex scenarios. These short reports contributed to the 'webs of significance which people weave within the cultural context, and these webs of significance can only be communicated to others by thickly describing the situation and its context' (Harvey and Myers, 2002). This process was valuable in exploring the perspectives of the different participants and resolving some element of the complexity of the layers of meaning recognizing that 'what we call our data are really our own constructions of other peoples constructions of what they and their compatriots are up to' (Walsham, 2002: p. 102).

The approach at this stage continued to be hermeneutic. It was valuable to continue to switch the focus between the detail of specific projects and the wider organizational context and between specific cases and the overall research. Lee (1999a: p. 19) refers to work by Kuhn and Rosabeth Moss Kanter to suggest that 'people know what they're doing', and that it is important to look at apparent absurdities and try to make sense of them. Lee suggests that when you do this it is important to look at what previously made sense and see if the meaning has changed.

Action research

Action research aims to solve practical problems while expanding scientific knowledge.

Unlike other research methods, where the researcher seeks to study organizational phenomena but not to change them, the action researcher is concerned to create organizational change and simultaneously to study the process. It is strongly oriented toward collaboration and change involving both researchers and subjects. Typically, it is an iterative research process that capitalizes on learning by both researchers and subjects within the context of the subjects' social system. It is a clinical method that puts IS researchers in a helping role with practitioners. (Baskerville and Myers, 2004: pp. 329–330)

There are many different varieties of action research and many different ways of approaching the design and execution of action research projects. Gummesson (2000: p. 16) positions action research as 'the most demanding and far-reaching method of doing case study research'.

Why use action research?

There are a number of good reasons for using an action research approach:

- 'The best way to learn about an organization is by attempting to change it' (Eden and Huxham, 1996: p. 82).
- 'Action research is one of the few valid research approaches that researchers can legitimately employ to study the effects of specific alterations in systems development methodologies. It is both rigorous and relevant' (Baskerville and Wood-Harper, 2002: pp. 137–138; I extend this to include methods related to change). The research project has a direct (and hopefully beneficial) impact on the organization.
- The participative and collaborative nature of the approach builds good engagement between practitioners and researchers which contributes to deeper insight and better research outcomes: and helps to equip participants with research competences which contribute to individual and organizational development (e.g. as reflective practitioners – Schon, 1983).

The main reason for NOT using action research is that it is time consuming and hard work. From a purely academic point of view it can also be harder to get published in highly ranked journals, although it is clearly recognized as a valid and important research method as demonstrated by the 2004 special issue of *MIS Quarterly* devoted to action research.

What is action research?

> Action research simultaneously assists in practical problem solving and expands scientific knowledge, as well as enhancing the competencies of the respective actors, being performed collaboratively in an immediate situation using data feedback in a cyclical process aiming at an increased understanding of a given social situation, primarily applicable to the understanding of change processes and undertaken within a mutually acceptable ethical framework. (Hult and Lennung, 1980 in Baskerville and Wood-Harper, 1996: p. 135)

The definition highlights the three intended outcomes of contribution to practice and theory, and the development of the competences of the participants.

The action taken can result in 'first order' change, that is an improvement in what the organization does or how it does it; or 'second order change' – 'a system-wide change in the nature of the core assumptions and ways of thinking and acting' (Coghlan and Brannick, 2005: p. 94; cf Argyris and ideas of single and double loop learning).

Checkland and Holwell (1998: pp. 22–28) present action research as a cyclical process. They stress the importance of establishing research themes and being guided by a framework of ideas (theory). This theoretical foundation distinguishes action research from consulting. The cycle can be entered at any point. A starting point is to establish a framework of ideas – this can be research themes or 'theory' based on relevant literature. This is followed by entering into a real-world 'problem situation' and taking action in the situation. This enables reflection based on the involvement and the research framework. Reflection leads to findings: new insights and to ideas and issues for a further cycle of research and learning.

I think that a key point, stressed by Checkland (Checkland and Holwell, 1998: pp. 22–27), is the need to understand the problem situation (diagnosis) before leaping into action and potentially using an inappropriate 'solution' or solving the 'wrong problem'. The use of theory, Checkland's framework of ideas, is designed to assist with diagnosis and solution definition. Checkland's work on Soft Systems (Checkland and Holwell, 1998) provides an extremely valuable way to explore different perspectives on a 'problematic situation' and to consider opportunities for improvements.

A research proposal may form a first action research cycle. This would typically include enough consideration of literature to frame the problem (Herr and Anderson, 2005: p. 71) and would not include a complete literature review, as in a positivist research project with a quantitative methodology. Further work on literature would take place as the research progressed through a number of cycles.

Roles in action research

The roles of the researcher(s) and research 'subjects' are a key consideration in the planning and execution of action research. For example, is the researcher an outsider who is coming into a situation as an expert and consultant with other research participants being 'subjects' with the research being *done* to them? While this is a possible scenario, it is not ideal: 'action research is best done in collaboration with others who have a stake in the problem under investigation' (Herr and Anderson, 2005: p. 4).

Coghlan and Brannick (2005: p. 8) refer to work by Reason and Bradbury and the *three voices* and audiences of 'action research – first, second and third person'. First person is the individual, and their development of an enquiring approach (cf reflective practitioner). Second person is 'us', the participants in the research seeking to learn and improve practice. The third person is the traditional perspective, for example the communication of research to others. They suggest that good research should reflect these three voices and audiences.

One of the advantages of action research is that it can be carried out by the individual on their own practice, their team or their organization. The research can be done by an individual or in collaboration with other 'insiders' or 'outsiders' (Herr and Anderson, 2005: p. 31). Depending on the approach taken, research participants are not 'subjects' but full 'collaborators.'

'Insider' action research brings a number of challenges and ethical considerations. For example, action research may challenge implicit, taken-for-granted assumptions within the organization and this is likely to meet resistance. There may also be concerns about the motives of the researchers and what will happen to any data gathered; for example, in a meeting how is the individual combining their role as a participant and as a researcher. Being an insider also has important advantages including ease of access to people and documents, opportunities for informal contacts, and a deep understanding of the content and problematic situation. Just as in case studies and ethnographic research, precautions have to be taken against the researcher 'going native' and losing objectivity. The research design has to take into account the need for the researchers to reflect on the situation and approach it in new ways, for example seeing the taken-for-granted aspects of their practice.

The action researcher as 'insider' is often an important element of action research and should be an important element of the conduct and communication of the research. Herr and Anderson (2005: p. 47) stress that action research should not be presented purely in the third person: 'To downplay or fail to acknowledge one's insider status is deceptive and allows the researcher to avoid the kind of intense self-reflection that is the hallmark of good practitioner research.'

Adopting an agile approach to research projects

In this section I focus on the *process* of research and the extent to which the research *process* is well aligned to the goal of transforming research into practice. To a large extent I want to avoid the debate about research *methods* as the qualitative vs quantitative and positivist vs interpretive conflicts have been covered in much detail elsewhere. I intend to explore the relevance of an *agile* approach to research projects. I draw on www.agilemanifesto.org, which provides an excellent summary of agile thinking. This is also developed in Agile Project Management (Highsmith, 2004). The manifesto provides a stark contrast with the focus on 'organisation and control' of PRINCE2 (www.prince2.com/prince2-structure.asp).

I first discovered agile approaches when I moved to Microsoft in 1998. The Microsoft Solutions Framework, developed before many well known agile approaches, embodied the key agile principles. It was a revelation how it provided an effective framework for consultants from around the world to rapidly form effective teams and to work together to deliver substantial solutions in short periods of time.

A range of specific practices can be adopted to implement an agile approach, these include:

- **Time boxing**: often interpreted as using small teams to deliver to fixed deadlines.
- **Versioned release**: delivering an overall solution through a series of rapid, time-boxed projects ('Deliver working software frequently, from a couple of weeks to a couple of months, with a preference to the shorter timescale') (the Agile Manifesto – see, for example, Highsmith, 2004).
- **Succeeding through multidisciplinary, collocated teams, working together effectively**: success through effective teamwork is covered by many of the agile principles, for example 'Business people and developers must work together daily throughout the project'; 'Build projects around motivated individuals. Give them the environment and support they need, and trust them to get the job done'; and 'The most efficient and effective method of conveying information to and within a development team is face-to-face conversation (the Agile Manifesto – see, for example, Highsmith, 2004).'
- **Efficient processes focused on the end goals**: work is required to adapt the agile principles to the research context: 'Working software is the primary measure of progress' and 'Simplicity – the art of maximizing the amount of work not done – is essential.'
- **Learning lessons about effective working**: there is a strong emphasis on ongoing learning by the research team: 'At regular intervals, the team reflects on how to become more effective, then tunes and adjusts its behaviour accordingly (the Agile Manifesto – see, for example, Highsmith, 2004).'

I have used two of my own research projects to explore the value of the agile principles for helping adjust our approach to research to increase the relevance to practice. First, one of the three in-depth case studies and secondly a much shorter project where I carried out a case study with a colleague to develop a conference paper. These projects are presented as brief 'vignettes' to illustrate the discussion.

Project 1: in-depth case study carried out as part of the empirical work for my PhD

The research was exploring the extent to which organizations have adopted benefits-driven practices when undertaking investments in IT. This case study involved a City Council. Semi-structured interviews, 12 in total, explored three specific projects and the organizational context in which the projects were taking place.

I had two initial meetings with a senior manager who agreed to be the organizational sponsor of the research. This resulted in agreement on which projects to study, identified specific individuals to talk to, and communication of his support for the research to interviewees. Following Silverman (2000) I started analysing the results of the interviews from day one of the fieldwork. As a result, I was able to prepare a brief summary of the findings from the case study in the form of a set of PowerPoint slides to discuss with the sponsor at a meeting within a few days of the last interview. This meeting took place on 18 October 2005. This was an extremely valuable meeting and helped me to understand more of *what* was happening and particularly *why* things were happening. During late 2006, I wrote and had published several short pieces in *Computer Weekly* and other practitioner magazines that were based on my PhD, including the findings from the case study. I prepared a first draft of a dissertation chapter discussing the case within a few weeks of completing the fieldwork but did not finalize the dissertation itself until October 2007 as I was working on it part time. It was at this point that I started writing for publication based on the dissertation and have since had a conference paper accepted based on the case (British Academy of Management, 2008).

In many respects the fieldwork was agile, with involvement of the sponsor at the beginning and end of the work. These meetings played an important role in the development of the overall PhD because of the amount of learning for me from engagement with this organization. Unfortunately, the long gap between completion of the fieldwork and completion of the PhD has resulted in a lack of communication with the organization. However, from a research perspective, the overall findings have evolved significantly because of the cross-case analysis and further reflection during the iterative process of writing up and further analysis.

Project 2: developing the information systems capability of the organization – a case study

The second research project followed on from the results of the PhD. Through a friend and colleague, Alison Freer (www.leadandtransformit.com), and as a result of a presentation I had done on Benefits Management at a local IT Directors Forum, I had the opportunity to carry out a case study of changes to an IT function as part of their project with the wider objective of developing the IS capability of the organization. We carried out all aspects of the work together. Her background, in executive coaching and personal development, and her contacts in the organization were invaluable.

An initial meeting with the IT manager, to discuss and agree the work, took place on 13 February 2008. The work was designed as a 'lessons learned review' to help the organization to identify what was going well, help establish the practice of reviewing lessons learned, and to encourage the sharing of successful practices. It was valuable to have the opportunity to explore the development of the IT capability of the organization from the perspective of multiple interviewees. With the IT Managers support, we carried out a series of interviews on 12 March and 3 April (12 in total). The core findings were written up within a few days and a draft paper was completed within four weeks. Due to holidays, and our mistake in not scheduling the meeting until the fieldwork was completed, we did not meet the IT Manager and HR Director to review our findings and complete the research with the organization until 9 June.

With better scheduling, and holidays permitting, we could have had the final meeting in mid-May rather than June. But, in any case, we had to schedule the work around other commitments, teaching in my case. The work was agile in a number of senses: it was focused on value for the customer; we were able to design it so that the customer was involved in the learning; and the interviews were structured as a 'lessons learned' review, and interviewees (individuals and small groups) commented how helpful it had been to take the time to reflect. In this case the multidisciplinary research team was also valuable. Our individual perspectives, broadly characterized as a focus on organizational change and a focus on individual change, were both relevant and were needed to explore some complex aspects of the case. Without both these viewpoints, and our joint involvement throughout the project, both the feedback to the customer and the academic results of the case would have been impoverished.

Lessons learned

I think the second project shows the value of a number of agile principles and practices for research projects. We certainly now have confidence that we can carry out a case study to produce worthwhile academic results and produce value to the organization in timescales that are suited to the pace of activity in a modern organizational setting. We have also seen the value of multidisciplinary teamwork in planning and carrying out the research. In addition, we have started to evolve an effective and repeatable way of working that we hope to refine further in a second case study. Meetings in a coffee shop near the organization form a vital part of this which provided the face-to-face conversations that form a key part of an agile approach. In both projects we had customer involvement, and particularly in the second project the research was designed to directly benefit the customer.

A key learning point for us is to explore the opportunity to involve the customer more directly throughout the process in design, evaluation and reporting. We can see that the results would have been developed further through a deeper process of shared learning, and that our research approach could then have been embedded more deeply in the customer so that they could more effectively repeat the lessons learned process.

Implications for further work

The agile, participative, action research approach evolving through this work provides a good basis for further work. Specifically, it encourages practitioner engagement through the alignment with reflective practice and benefits for participants.

In concluding I go back to the beginning, and look to Geoff Walsham for advice: 'I take an interpretive study to mean that multiple perceptions are provided by participants, and thus that the interesting data from the study cannot be "triangulated" to provide "true" interpretations, since which truth would be chosen? The interpretive researcher filters participants' statements and actions through the lens of his or her own subjectivity, and then produces a "story" about the events that have occurred and some reasons for them. The purpose of the story, again is not to tell "the truth" about the case study but to tell "a truth", namely the researcher's own thoughts and ideas concerning the phenomena at issue' (Walsham, 2001: p. 7).

13
Looking Ahead – Implications and Opportunities

In the final chapter, I will set out the implications of the work for policy and practice *and set out future research directions.*

Progress so far

The original work on Benefits Management (Ward et al., 1996) was driven by practitioner needs and was carried out with significant practitioner involvement. The driver for this research was to contribute to management practice and the guiding philosophy was the participatory paradigm (Breu and Peppard, 2003). As Lyttinen (1999) comments a significant contribution to practice is typically beyond the scope of a PhD study: 'My experience shows that it takes at least three to five years to do anything. Thus anything that really addresses relevant concerns is beyond the scope of a single Ph.D. study.' The projects that support this book took place over an eight-year period and draw on strong foundations in earlier work by others. The ongoing research has a number of implications for managerial practice.

An initial implication is the value of a focus on developing organizational IS competences for benefits realization. This represents a major shift in perspective for many organizations who have attempted to implement new methods, methodologies and tools to improve their success with projects and have focused on the IT function. The competences perspective emphasizes that making an improvement should be a benefit driven change programme affecting the whole organization.

A further implication is based on the value of practices, which in line with the perspective on dynamic capabilities provided by Eisenhardt and Martin (2000) shows a strong degree of consistency across organizations. The practices developed require further research, but at a practitioner level are very well supported. They provide a basis for making phased and incremental improvements, starting by addressing the specific circumstances of a particular project or organization. The fit of the approach with how people actually work suggests it is a valuable way to make improvements.

The practices and competences approach reflects that there is no single best way for an organization to approach realizing value from IT and that the approach must be adapted to the specific circumstances of the organization. This research has provided one example of a very successful organization, which provides a number of features that are likely to be of wide applicability to other organizations. One specific feature is the phased development of competences, supported by the incremental adoption of a toolkit for change (framework of practices). In particular, the case showed a great value in education and development of people and in getting the basics right before moving on. Part of their success can be seen in the principles put forward by Lee (1999a) – the instantiation of the new 'intellectual technology', the change framework, resulted in changes to the organization, which in turn affected the further development of the technology. Specifically they found that education based on core elements of PRINCE2, the consistent use of elements including risk management and lessons learned, resulted in cultural changes to allow more open communication and a greater openness to learning.

Although there is no single best way to address developing competences for benefits realization, there are strong indications from the research of the value of practices and that they can be shared between organizations. There are also indications of a maturity process as organizations go through recognizable stages in the development of competence. One participant in the research talked about 'playbooks' for mergers and acquisitions. The idea recognized that no two acquisitions are the same, but they fall into a number of patterns and that there is much to gain from recognizing the similarity and adopting a relevant approach – that is, the playbook. I speculate that this concept will be valuable and hope to test it out and evolve different 'playbooks' for competence development through further research.

Practical implications

At the level of a specific project or investment in IT, there are a number of implications of the research for managerial practice. A number of changes are required, which, for organizations that have already adopted agile approaches, should not be significant. However, the change in perspective from solution delivery to benefits realization through changes to people, process and technology represents a paradigm shift, which for many individuals and organizations is a major challenge. Introduction of a benefits approach in the absence of this shift may only result in following a new set of rules without real change in the understanding and behaviour of individuals. Making this paradigm shift is potentially a critical factor in developing the benefits realization capability of an organization. A specific barrier to change is the adherence of most of the IT industry and project management profession to the old paradigm. In addition, there is only limited brand recognition for benefits management and other socio-technical approaches – PRINCE2, CMMI and other traditional approaches are still seen as the answer.

In summary, developing organizational competences for benefits realization is a process of organizational change that is likely to require a strategic initiative over a period of time. There is likely to be a maturity effect and organizations will need to continue to adopt new practices over a period of time (phased approach) as they gradually develop a benefits realization capability.

Work on the barriers to adoption of benefits-driven approaches (Chapter 8) and action research to develop the benefits realization capability of an organization (Chapter 11) have provided a number of insights. The implications of this research for practitioners are that important factors that contribute to the development of a benefits realization capability include:

- Phased adoption of practices for benefits realization.
- Phased development of organizational competences for benefits realization.
- Adherence to a set of *principles* that represent a focus on benefits delivery. Adoption of these principles will represent a 'paradigm shift' for many organizations and is a major issue. The extent of

change involved may mean that new structures and roles are required.

- Establishing an overall project *framework* that provides a basis for the different stakeholders to work together and bring the various competences together.
- Ownership and leadership for development of the benefits realization capability, supported by the ability to provide coaching and advice to people involved in project teams.
- An educational programme based on the practices and competences, underpinned by the principles and an overall framework for a project.
- An ability to learn and improve, enabled by sharing practices within the organization, potentially through relevant 'toolkits' (pattern languages) used by communities of practice.

Work addressing the gap between the business and the IT function addresses aspects of this issue from a different perspective and it would be valuable to explore this further in future research (Taylor-Cummings, 1998; Peppard and Ward, 1999; Peppard, 2001).

The area of Benefits Exploitation has emerged as a major issue at a number of stages of the research. In our recent project, Exploring Business Transformation (Chapter 6) that involved 65 interviews with business and IT managers from a very wide range of organizations, we covered the area of Benefits Exploitation. Very often, it is left to chance: *'end users of systems lack knowledge – it's a case of loss of knowledge through staff turnover and passing on knowledge informally from one to the other'* (Business manager, financial services). The knowledge of what is possible and how to realize the full potential of the new technology is quickly fragmented and lost. When many organizations are still using systems 20 or more years old, this is an important area. This view was reinforced in our recent survey of senior business managers where exploitation of existing systems and information was the area of lowest satisfaction when we explored benefits from IT.

Benefits Exploitation goes beyond the end date of most projects – all too often, the project ends at the technology live date plus 7 or 14 days. The team is disbanded and they move onto new projects or new customers just when they are needed most, just when everything they have learnt can really add value. Benefits Exploitation tackles the crucial post-live period when huge amounts of learning occur and when a continued focus on benefits realization is essential. It continues to provide a focus on benefits through the lifecycle of a system.

Practices for Benefits Exploitation are not well established. Our paper on knowledge worker productivity (see Appendix 1) provides some coverage of this important area. The key message is that there are significant opportunities for many organizations and large investments are *not* required to make a difference.

A final practical implication to emphasize is the importance of the skills of individuals and teams. This was highlighted very strongly in the action research project (Chapter 11), where a key contribution of the benefits practices was as an enabler of communication and creative, effective ways of working. They provide a common language and contribute to the development of a benefits 'mindset'. I feel this is a crucial point for other organizations if they are to avoid the risks of failing with a benefits-driven approach through turning it into a new project bureaucracy.

Policy and wider implications

Business leadership for benefits realization

Research has identified an 'IT attention deficit' at Board level (Huff and Maher, 2006). To explore this further I carried out a survey between December 2009 and February 2010 to get the views of senior business managers on the question: 'have organizations got the leadership capabilities to realize the strategic potential of information systems?' Of the 117 responses, 55 per cent were from Board level management and 75 per cent were from senior business and IT management.

The survey results suggest that Information Technology (IT) is critical to day-to-day operations and is a key contributor to current and future sources of competitive advantage (94% of 117 respondents). IT also makes an important contribution to cost reduction and improving efficiency (70% were satisfied or very satisfied).

IT risk is taken into consideration by senior management (69%). But, it is a concern that in only 27 per cent of cases did senior management take action to obtain information on IT trends and new business opportunities enabled by IT. This contrasts with the strategic role of IT.

There was strong evidence of the barrier between business and IT: only 29 per cent agreed or strongly agreed that senior business and IT managers speak the same language. So, even if there is some IT presence in the boardroom there is a wider problem of communication.

Based on all the responses, the survey indicates that senior management have expertise in IT strategy and project delivery (44%). The view from senior IT managers is less positive, in fact, only 12 per cent agree that senior business management have expertise in these areas. Only 26 per cent agreed that leadership development activities currently address business manager engagement in IT strategy and project sponsorship. So there is also evidence of a need for action to develop skills in this area.

There are crucial issues here. IT is critical to business success, but there is only limited focus on future strategic opportunities. There is limited focus on developing the leadership capabilities required to realize the strategic potential of IT. Above all, there is a language barrier between senior business and IT management, which makes it hard to tackle any of the other issues.

The focus on benefits realization provides principles, a common framework and language, as well as specific practices that enable business leadership for benefits realization from IT.

Business education

Many of the elements of an effective approach to IT have been established, but they have not become widely adopted and used in practice. *There is a significant 'knowing–doing' gap.* Business and management education is one lever to pull to try to bridge the gap.

Previous work in this area has largely focused on the need for the coverage of IS in MBA programmes and developing an improved syllabus. By taking the goal of education as conceptual change and organizational development a much broader view is taken of the actions required to bridge the gap between what we know and what happens in practice. Areas for action include:

- Building IS educational programmes around a core of successful practices for realizing benefits from IS.

- Focusing on the underlying philosophy in education and guiding principles for succeeding with IS as well as specific knowledge and techniques.
- Providing a much broader range of educational and advisory support to enable individuals and organizations to continue to learn and to put their learning into practice.

In addition a paradigm shift is required to break out of the existing IS paradigm (success through improved project methods or better software engineering) and shift to a new paradigm (success through a focus on benefits realization from organizational change and effective teamwork).

A key implication is that there is a major role for business education to help to bring about these changes and to help to equip organizations to realize the potential of IT. There is a long way to go – IT or benefits from IT-enabled change is often absent from the curriculum or has a techno-centric focus. The reward for organizations that can bridge the 'knowing–doing' gap will be substantial.

Public sector

We know that the failure rate of IT projects is high and that failures in the public sector tend to get a lot of publicity. Many factors contribute to the well-documented failures and huge sums of money wasted, particularly in government projects. It has been frustrating to see a number of attempts to adopt benefits-driven approaches fail as the focus has been on imposing a methodology rather than building up skills. There is also a stubborn adherence to a techno-centric mindset and over emphasis on IT procurement.

Benefits-driven approaches are a natural fit with a public service ethos of value for stakeholders and value for money. Leadership for the development of benefits realization competences in public sector organizations is essential. It is vital to recognize that this goes beyond the current emphasis on PRINCE2 and Managing Successful Programmes.

Looking ahead

There are many opportunities for further research to contribute to the ability of individuals and organizations to realize the strategic potential of IT. A number of promising areas are outlined in this section. First, work on dynamic capabilities is a major strand of strategic management research. Benefits realization from IT relates to both the dynamic and substantive capabilities of an organization. There is an opportunity to take advantage of the development of thinking on dynamic capabilities to gain fresh insights into benefits realization. The discussion makes a first attempt to reinterpret findings to date through the lens of dynamic capabilities.

A second important theme is the role of IT as an enabler of business innovation. Many aspects of the research to date can enable innovation. There are also opportunities to build on insights from the large literature on innovation including merging work on 'design thinking' (Brown, 2008). The final theme is 'craft' and the role of the craftsman as a way of exploring developing competences.

Work by others, for example, on IT architecture and the role of the CIO, will also make a valuable contribution.

Dynamic capability

Many practices that contribute to successful realization of benefits from IT have been identified. The primary problem is that they are not widely, consistently and effectively adopted (BCS, 2004). In an initial report of our research (Ashurst et al., 2008) we explored the challenges of realizing benefits from investments in IT from a resource-based perspective, and developed a model of an organizational benefits realization capability and a framework of practices for benefits realization. In this section, we explore the implications of previous work on dynamic capabilities for our understanding of benefits realization, and the development and effectiveness of a benefits realization capability.

The resource-based view of the firm has become a major strand of strategic management research and, as a result, provides an important starting point when considering the realization of value from IT: 'The theoretical and practical importance of developing and applying dynamic capabilities to sustain a firms' competitive advantage in complex, and volatile external environments has catapulted this issue to the research agenda of many scholars' (Zahra et al., 2006). An increasing number of authors have considered the concept of the 'dynamic capabilities' of an organization (Ambrosini and Bowman, 2009).

The idea of a 'dynamic capability' can be traced back to early work by Teece and then to Penrose and Schumpeter: 'the mechanisms by which firms learn and accumulate new skills and capabilities and the forces that limit the rate and direction of this process' (Teece et al., 1990). The concept is being developed and explored in the strategic management literature. Dynamic capabilities can also be defined as:

> The firm's processes that use resources – specifically the processes to integrate, reconfigure, gain and release resources – to match and even create market change. Dynamic capabilities thus are the organizational and strategic routines by which firms achieve new resource configurations as markets emerge, collide, split, evolve, and die. (Eisenhardt and Martin, 2000)

Zahra et al. (2006) refer to a dynamic capability as the 'dynamic capability to change or reconfigure existing substantive capabilities'. This requires a definition of *substantive* capabilities, which they give as 'the ability to solve a problem' (p. 921). A dynamic capability is the ability to change the way a 'firm solves its problems'. If an organization does not have or use dynamic capabilities, any advantage from substantive capabilities may be short lived due to changes in the environment or competitor action.

A dynamic capability has some patterned element; it is repeatable (Zollo and Winter, 2002). Also dynamic capabilities are not synonymous with strategic change; for example, changes may occur through adhoc interventions, through emergent processes that have not been deployed by managers, or by luck (Ambrosini and Bowman, 2009). There is also room for some exploration of what represents a dynamic capability in a particular organization: differing from Eisenhardt and Martin (2000), Zahra et al. (2006) see new product development as a substantive capability, and the ability to change how the firm develops new products as a dynamic capability (p. 921).

Bowman and Ambrosini (2003) explain that dynamic capabilities comprise four main processes (examples omitted):

- 'Reconfiguration: transformation and recombination of assets and resources

- Leveraging: replicating a process or system that is operating in one business unit into another, or extending a resource by deploying it into a new domain
- Learning: to perform tasks more effectively and efficiently as an outcome of experimentation, reflecting on failure and success
- Creative integration: ability to integrate assets and resources resulting in a new resource configuration'.

In addition (Augier and Teece, 2008; Teece, 2007),

- 'Search – identifying opportunities & threats
- Sensing – changing customer requirements'.

'Organizations realize value from their dynamic capabilities in the choices they make in how they are applied to develop new or improved "substantive capabilities"' (Zahra et al., 2006). Value is then realized through the resulting substantive capabilities. This parallels the way value is realized from IT, with the direct impact being on business process performance, which in turn contributes to improved organizational performance (Melville et al., 2004) As a result a key contributor to realizing value from dynamic capabilities is the 'entrepreneurial alertness' (Sambamurthy and Bharadwaj, 2003) that helps an organization to recognize the opportunities and take action. Lockett (2005) builds on work by Penrose and emphasizes the need for entrepreneurial skills including imagination to contribute to change and gaining competitive advantage and not just managerial competence of running the current business.

In order to make good decisions about how to apply dynamic capabilities, management need to be able to consider a range of possible futures and assess the value that can be realized (Amit and Schoemaker, 1993; Srivastava et al., 2001). Zahra et al. (2006) relate this ability to the level of knowledge of the organization. There is also a risk that options are ignored because of a lack of knowledge or overlooked because of an inability to see beyond the current frame or paradigm (Eisenhardt and Martin, 2000). In addition, as Sambamurthy and Bharadwaj note (2003), value is provided by the 'digital options' represented by investments in business and IT substantive capabilities that open up new possibilities not planned at the time of the original investment. These options contribute to agility, which is extremely important in a changing and unpredictable business environment. Teece et al. (1997) also note that there are situations where local autonomy to allow a decentralized approach to change may be important.

Organizational capabilities, both dynamic and substantive capabilities, are developed through learning and application (Powell and Dent-Micallef, 1997, Prahalad and Hamel, 1990, Grant, 1996a). Zollo and Winter (2002: p. 344) suggest, 'dynamic capabilities emerge from the co-evolution of tacit experience accumulation processes with explicit knowledge articulation and codification activities'. Ambrosini and Bowman (2009) refer to the importance of social capital, particularly individuals' internal and external social ties to enable information sharing and contribute to innovation.

There is also a risk of decay or loss of capabilities through lack of use and substantive capabilities may become difficult to change if they are left unchanged for a period of time (Eisenhardt and Martin, 2000). Dynamic capabilities are built rather than bought in the market. The development of dynamic capabilities is path dependent and it is likely that there is a natural sequence of development (Eisenhardt and Martin, 2000). They also suggest that they are 'equifinal'. As a specific example, Ross (2003) notes that the development of IT architecture capabilities must be in stages and it is very unlikely that an organization will be successful if it tries to miss out a stage of development. The ability to learn, and to develop dynamic capabilities, is in itself a higher-order dynamic capability (Ambrosini and Bowman, 2009). Developing and maintaining dynamic capabilities is expensive (Zollo and Winter, 2002; Winter, 2003, Ambrosini and Bowman, 2009).

The dynamic capability requires a range of individuals with different knowledge and skills working together in multidisciplinary, cross-functional teams. To be effective there is a need for a common language and some level of common experience and common process (sequencing, rules and directives) (Eisenhardt and Martin, 2000; Grant, 1996b). In addition, as Grant notes (1996b), 'rules and directives' and group problem solving are important in the effectiveness of this knowledge-intensive work. The degree of codification of the routines that is helpful will vary according to the velocity of markets

(Eisenhardt and Martin, 2000). Similarly, Bohn (1994) explores the appropriate degree of proceduralization depending on the level of knowledge of a business process.

As we have noted (Ashurst et al., 2008), these routines are practices, representing the work people do. They can be the basis for establishing a common approach, or a specific way of working as part of a substantive or dynamic organizational capability. These practices, which contribute to a capability, can be shared within an organization and between organizations. As Teece et al. (1997) indicate there is value in inter-organizational learning.

Practices provide a way to tackle issues raised by Delbridge et al. (2006); they focus on the 'black box' of productive performance and provide a specific mechanism to translate inputs into productive activity. They also provide a potential way to connect an investment in skills into a contribution to improved productivity by helping shape what people do in the workplace. Research has suggested that the adoption of practices needs to be approached as a strategic change programme and in many cases it is not (Leseure et al., 2004). One of the barriers to adoption of practices for business transformation is lack of awareness of a need and as a result a lack of demand for adoption. This is an example of a more general issue affecting the sharing of knowledge (Bessant et al., 2005). In the terms used by Siebers et al. (2008), there is often a lack of 'needs pull'. This could related to the point made by Eisenhardt and Martin (2000), using the example of acquisitions, that there is a need for some level of initial knowledge, so that more advanced knowledge can be developed through a variety of experience.

This is an important area for further research. As Prahalad and Hamel (1990) note, there should be more management focus on planning for the development of core competences rather than just on financial budgeting. In addition, Peppard and Ward (2004) note that there is a need for further research on how to develop competences.

Ambrosini and Bowman (2009: p. 37) state that there is a need for further empirical studies and particularly qualitative studies to understand the 'mechanisms of how these capabilities are deployed or how they "work"' and so that guidance for managers can be developed (Box 13.1).

Box 13.1   Key questions for further research (Ambrosini and Bowman, 2009)

'We have little theoretical or empirical evidence as to how dynamic capabilities can be deliberately built' (P44), also if they are commonly found within an industry and not differentiated across firms might they be 'relatively easy to build'? (P44).

The level of similarity may relate to how high level a perspective is taken we might expect 'subtle, but important differences between firms' (P44).

Things we are still unclear about 'how dynamic capabilities are created' (P45) – so that we can develop guidance for managers'.

What dynamic capabilities look like in organizations, how they are deployed, whether and how they differ across firms (P46).

Our initial research has made a number of contributions in relation to the adoption and effective application of practices to contribute to the successful realization of benefits from IT in organizations. It established a framework of practices for benefits realization, which can be further developed and refined. It also supported the value of the practice 'lens' from research and practitioner perspectives. Practices appear to be a good fit with how people work and provide a good basis for sharing knowledge. This alignment with how people actually work suggests that the practices perspective taken for this research has the potential to make an impact on what actually happens in organizations. Recent research by Ward et al. (2007) provides evidence of the importance of practices and their link with IS project success. In addition, our research provided insights into the factors inhibiting the adoption of benefits-driven approaches.

The benefits realization capability is the means by which an organization realizes value from IT. The capability is organization-wide, not just embedded in the IT function (Bharadwaj, 2000; Peppard and Ward, 2004; Peppard, 2007). The capability has transformational (dynamic) and operational elements (Ravichandran, T. and Lertwongsatien, 2005). Value realization depends on fusing IT with complementary, firm specific, human and business resources (Powell et al., 1997). Value is realized from both the dynamic and substantive elements of the benefits realization capability. The 'greatest gains come from doing the right things' (Earl and Feeny, 1994): the strategic choices (Ward and Peppard, 2004) that are the result of entrepreneurial alertness, and activities (Sambamurthy and Bharadwaj, 2003) lead to value being realized when dynamic capabilities are deployed within the business to establish new or improved substantive capabilities. The operational (substantive) element of the benefits realization capability includes the exploitation of IT to contribute to value creation as part of wider, substantive business capabilities. In the research, we consider the value of the practices perspective to both dynamic and substantive elements of the benefits realization capability (and explore the importance of different degrees of codification related to the velocity of markets and other factors (Eisenhardt and Martin).

In summary key propositions from work on dynamic capabilities that relate to our work on developing the benefits realization capability of an organization include the following:

- There are substantive and dynamic elements to the benefits realization capability.
- It is organization-wide.
- Value from the dynamic aspects of the capability depends on the choices made as to how it is applied. Making the right decisions depends on insight into possible futures and on being able to see beyond the frame of the current situation.
- Value from IT is realized in conjunction with complementary business and human resources as part of both substantive and dynamic capabilities.
- Practices are an important contributor to organizational capabilities. The practices that contribute to dynamic capabilities have much in common across organizations.
- Practices can be codified to an extent, and the level of codification which is valuable will differ depending on the velocity of the market.
- There are times when completely new capabilities are needed – organizations must watch out for this as they could get stuck by their expertise in old, irrelevant ways of doing things.
- Routines (practices) are part of a wider approach to effective working in a knowledge-intensive environment. Wider factors include establishing a common language, a framework provided by rules,

directives and sequencing; effective teamwork including group decision-making and problem-solving.

- Capabilities are developed through intra- and inter-organizational learning and from learning by doing.
- There is at last some element of a natural sequence of adoption of practices. The path of development of a benefits realization capability will have some similarities across organizations.
- Adoption of new practices and competence development is a process of strategic change.
- Dynamic capabilities and the changes they result in are costly and the level of change/capability required will vary. The cost of change will decrease with experience (there may be limits?).
- Different substantive capabilities may need different dynamic capabilities to succeed with change (Zahra et al.: p. 947).
- Finally, the lack of focus on building dynamic capabilities (benefits realization capability) is an example of organizations/management being stuck in an outdated frame/paradigm and therefore being unable to see the need for a new way of doing things.

Grant (1996b) challenges the concept of organizational learning put forward by others including Garvin (1993) and suggests that individuals learn. An important aspect of the research is to consider these different perspectives and explore the development or adoption of new practices and how practices are sustained as the individuals involved change.

Work on dynamic capabilities provides a fresh look at a range of existing business and research areas. It has been valuable to use dynamic capabilities as a fresh lens on our work on benefits realization. In Table 13.1, evidence from the work to date is related to the propositions highlighted above. In general, the empirical evidence for the research provides good support for the propositions.

This initial review suggests that there is value in further work, exploring a dynamic capability perspective on benefits realization. The link may help to provide support for a greater focus on benefits realization. It also enables us to take advantage of the large body of research on dynamic capabilities to advance the work on benefits realization.

Table 13.1 Implications of dynamic capabilities for benefits realization: findings from empirical work

Proposition based on previous work on dynamic capabilities	Empirical findings from the research programme
There are substantive and dynamic elements to the benefits realization capability.	The cases reported in Chapters 5 and 11 highlight organizations aiming to developing both elements of the capability. They also indicate a linkage as the dynamic capability evolves through changing substantive capabilities.
The benefits realization capability is organization-wide.	In Chapter 5, the organization is explicitly working to develop an organization-wide capability. The Benefits Planning competence addresses this area through a focus on benefits for stakeholders.
Value from the dynamic aspects of the capability depends on the choices made as to how it is applied. Making the right decisions depends on insight into possible futures and on being able to see beyond the frame of the current situation.	Evidence supporting this proposition is in the practices for portfolio management (Chapter 7), which show making the right decisions as a process of experimentation and learning. The benefits-driven approach, which provides the basis for the research, is built on this foundation.
Value from IT is realized in conjunction with complementary business and human resources as part of both substantive and dynamic capabilities	The cases highlight the importance of active business leadership to realize benefits.
Practices are an important contributor to organizational capabilities. The practices that contribute to dynamic capabilities have much in common across organizations. Practices can be codified to an extent, and the level of codification, which is valuable, will differ depending on the velocity of the market.	Many aspects of the work, for example the practice for portfolio management (Chapter 7), indicate the opportunities for sharing practices between organizations. Practices and patterns are proving valuable approaches to codification and sharing. Further evidence is required to explore their limitations, for example, in high-velocity situations. However, we note that the fit with agile approaches suggest that they are valuable in a very wide range of contexts.

Continued

Table 13.1   Continued

Proposition based on previous work on dynamic capabilities	Empirical findings from the research programme
There are times when completely new capabilities are needed – organizations must watch out for this as they could get stuck by their expertise in old, irrelevant ways of doing things.	This reflects the challenges to the adoption of benefits-driven approaches (Chapter 8), where organizations are stuck in a mindset of improving outdated approaches rather than taking a fresh approach.
Routines are part of a wider approach to effective working in a knowledge-intensive environment. Wider factors include establishing a common language, a framework provided by rules, directives and sequencing; effective teamwork including group decision-making and problem-solving.	Our work has highlighted a number of wider factors, for examples principles guiding benefits realization and the importance of a common language (Chapter 11). A further implication is that the same ideas (practices, principles) will be valuable in understanding the substantive capability that is being changed.
Capabilities are developed through intra- and inter-organizational learning and from learning by doing.	There is support for this proposition in many aspects of the research. It is explicit in the cases in Chapters 5 and 11.
There is at last some element of a natural sequence of adoption of practices/path of development of a benefits realization capability.	Phased adoption of practices and the existence of common patterns of development are indicated by the cases (Chapters 5 and 6).
Adoption of new practices is a process of strategic change.	The research reported in Chapter 11 is testing this out and provides clear support. The case also highlights the importance of leadership for the development of the benefits realization capability.
Dynamic capabilities and the changes they result in are costly and the level of change/capability required will vary. The cost of change will decrease with experience (there may be limits?).	Further work is certainly required. The case in Chapter 11 does support that significant effort is required over the long term.
Different substantive capabilities may need different dynamic capabilities to succeed with change (Zahra et al.: p. 947).	Further work is required. It is, however, well established in Chapter 7 (also previous IT research) that there is a clear value in adapting the approach to an IT project to suit the business context (i.e. the substantive capability).

Innovation and design

IT continues to provide many opportunities for business innovation. Many elements of the work to date at both project and portfolio level specifically take into account the need to succeed with benefits realization in scenarios where innovation is important. The ongoing action research (Chapter 11) has highlighted the vital role of creative and collaborative ways of working as enablers of benefits realization. The focus on value for the stakeholder fits directly with agile approaches to IT, which have contributed to, or at least reflect, the ideas of 'design thinking' (Brown, 2008).

There is a large body of academic work on innovation, and both innovation and design thinking are currently major areas of emphasis for many large organizations. A priority for further work on benefits realization is to make these links more explicit and draw on wider research and lessons learned.

From an IT attention deficit to IT savvy business management

The work to date has provided evidence of the 'IT Attention Deficit' and the value of the benefits approach in bridging the business–IT divide and helping to develop 'IT savvy' business leaders. This is an important area for further work. Further projects need to extend the work to focus more directly on business leaders and their development as leaders of benefits realization. One link to this would be through the role of the CIO as 'facilitator' put forward by Peppard et al. (2011).

Craft

Skilled enactment of practices for benefits realization emerged as a key emphasis at an early stage of the work. The link of practices with patterns as a way for professionals to capture and share knowledge reinforces this, as do many of the insights from agile approaches including the (self-)discipline of the team as opposed to the (imposed) control of management.

We have come to see strong links with ideas of craft and craftsman (Sennett, 2009). There are also strong links with Schon (1983) and reflective practice and the education of professionals. Key points are the need for 'learning by doing' (the apprenticeship of the craftsman) and that craftsmen are dedicated to *'good work for its own sake'*. ... their labour is not simply a means to another end (Sennett, 2009: p. 20). The goal here is benefits realization for stakeholders.

(I assume we have moved beyond the stage of having to refer to he/she.)

The tools of the craftsman are often deceptively simple, and can be used at a basic or an advanced level. Building competences is not just about introducing the tools; it is about helping individuals, teams and the wider organization to learn how and when to use them and developing expertise in their use. The expert probably has more tools available to them than the novice, but they certainly know how to use them very effectively in a wide range of situations. Our patterns representing practices for benefits realization are our tools as craftsmen.

A common reaction to the benefits approach is that it is (just) 'common sense'. However, common sense is clearly not common practice. I hope that the perspective of the development of craft skills will contribute to the shift from common sense to common (skilled) practice. It is not knowing about the tools that counts, it's using them effectively at the right times. This craft perspective will provide fresh insights into the development of individual and organizational competences as the work progresses.

Small organizations

Most of our work to date has been with medium and large organizations. The projects we have run with smaller organizations indicate that the same ideas are relevant but that priorities change. Technology skills and the costs of initial investments have been barriers to some. It will be interesting to see if and how new developments, such as Cloud, change this. The business change issues faced by large organizations have not been a problem in our work to date with small organizations. The key to success has been Benefits Planning: usually approached informally based on an entrepreneurial approach to spotting and acting on opportunities (Ashurst et al., 2011).

There are certainly opportunities to explore how best to support small organizations in the development of benefits realization capabilities.

Taking forward the work on building capabilities

The reported failure rate of investments in IT has remained high for decades. There is no reason to expect a rapid change. Building the capability of organizations to realize benefits from IT remains a critical challenge.

New technology developments (Cloud, broadband wifi, mobile devices, social media etc.) are making more powerful solutions and services available to many more individuals and organizations. These developments provide new business opportunities and influence the nature of technical challenges. They do not affect the core issues of benefits realization. In fact, the speed of change probably means that Brynjolfsson and Saunders (2009) are right and that the leaders, the more effective organizations, will be able to pull further away from the rest.

We view developing competences for benefits realization as primarily a challenge of bridging a major 'knowing–doing gap'. Success requires leadership and often a new mindset, as well as the gradual adoption of practices for benefits realization. Future research will build on findings to date with the aim of evolving guidance for organizations and helping them to assess the current situation and plan a change programme. We hope to develop a number of 'playbooks' that will enable sharing of learning of patterns for the development of competences for benefits realization.

Appendices

Appendix 1: outline of the research programme and related deliverables

Exploring the adoption of benefits-driven practices for IT investments (2004–6)

The project involved two phases of work. In total, there were case studies of IT projects across 45 organizations, principally from the UK, USA and Europe. The research discovered a very low level of adoption of benefits-driven practices. A framework of competences and practices for benefits realization was developed from this research (Chapter 4).

Ashurst, C. and Doherty, N.F. (2003) Establishing an organizational capability to succeed in realizing benefits from IT investments: An exploratory analysis. In Bergout, E and Remenyi (eds), Proceedings of the10th *European Conference on Information Technology Evaluation*, 1–11.

Ashurst, C. and Doherty, N.F. (2003a) Towards the formulation of a 'best practice framework for benefits realization in IT projects'. *Electronic Journal of Information Systems Evaluation*, 6, 2.

Ashurst, C., Doherty, N. and Peppard, J. (2008) Improving the impact of IT development projects: the benefits realization capability model. *European Journal of Information Systems* 17, pp. 352–370.

In-depth case studies: exploring the benefits realization capability (2005–7)

In-depth case studies of 3–4 projects were carried out in each of the three organizations. Interviews (10–20 in each organization) and a review of documentation covered the selected projects, and the wider business and IT environment in which they were taking place. The study provided support for the framework of competences and practices, highlighted a range of factors related to the IT portfolio, and provided insights into the challenges of developing the benefits realization capability of the organization. (Chapter 5 reports on one of the three organizations. Chapter 8 draws on all three organizations.)

Ashurst, C. (2008) Business transformation enabled by information systems: lessons from a case study of a City Council. Paper presented at the *British Academy of Management* conference.

Benefits toolkit: examples as workshop resources – available from research. ncl.ac.uk/transform/resources.php (**Benefits toolkit**: available from the author.)

Benefits realization competences and business innovation in an SME (2006–7)

Case study of three organizations. One of the cases forms the basis for the paper. (Not reported in detail in the book.)

Ashurst, C., Cragg, P. and Herring, P. (2011) The Role of IT Competences in Gaining Value from E-Business: an SME Case Study. *International Small Business Journal* (published online before print – March 2011). http://isb.sagepub.com/content/early/2011/03/10/0266242610375703.abstract (last accessed on 31 July 2011).

Exploring the value of patterns (2006–9)

A project with a number of colleagues at Durham exploring the value of patterns for project management. The project involved students in a 3rd-year-project management module acting as managers for teams of software developers on a second-year project. The research provides support for the value of patterns and insight into how to use them effectively. (Not reported in detail in the book.)

Hatch, A., Burd, E., Ashurst, C. and Jessop, A. (2007) Project management patterns and the research–teaching nexus. *Higher Education Academy* – subject centre conference.

Ashurst, C. (2008) Patterns of learning: enabling students to put knowledge into action. Paper accepted at the *Improving Student Learning* conference.

Burd, E.L., Hatch, A., Ashurst, C. and Jessop, A. (2009) Building project management communities: exploring the contribution of patterns supported by web 2.0 technologies. *Computer Science Education*, 19, pp. 257–272.

Exploring the challenges of benefits realization (2008–9)

The project explored the challenges affecting organizations seeking to realize benefits from IT investments and develop their benefits realization capability. Interviews and workshops included 65 business and IT managers. IT portfolio management emerged as a major theme and there was preliminary evidence of the development pathways taken by organization as they developed an IT portfolio management capability (Chapter 6).

Ashurst C and Hodges J. (2009) Exploring business transformation. Paper presented at the British Academy of Management conference.

Ashurst, C. and Hodges, J. (2010) Exploring business transformation: the challenges of developing a benefits realization capability. *Journal of Change Management*, 10, 2, pp. 217–237.

Business briefing available from the author.

Portfolio management practices (2009–10)

The project started with an in-depth case study of IT portfolio management in one organization. The work involved interviews with a number of directors and members of the IT management team (12 in all) and resulted in a preliminary framework of practices for IT portfolio management. A workshop session involving approximately 20 members of a regional IT Directors Forum provided an opportunity to test out and refine the ideas and specific practices.

Workshop session with members of the Russell Group IT Directors Forum (RUGIT) provided an opportunity to test out and refine the findings(Chapter 7).

Ashurst C. and Doherty, N. (2009) Developing the information systems capability of the organization: a portfolio perspective. Paper presented at the *UK Academy of Information Systems* Conference.

Business briefing available at research.ncl.ac.uk/transform/resources.php

Case study – assessment of benefits realization competences (2009–10)

The case study tested out the use of the framework of competences and practices as a diagnostic framework to identify priorities for action to develop the benefits realization capability of an organization. (Not reported in detail in the book.)

Straker, T. and Ashurst, C. (2010) Benefits realization in IS/IT projects: a case study. Paper presented at the UK Academy of Information Systems conference.

Is there an IT attention deficit in the North East of England? (2010)

Exploratory survey of IT and business leaders. (Not reported in detail in the book.)

Business briefing available at research.ncl.ac.uk/transform/resources.php

Improving knowledge worker productivity (2008–10)

Exploratory survey of IT and business leaders followed by a workshop with members of the IT Directors Forum. (Not reported in detail in the book.)

Ashurst, C. and Doig, G. (2005) Information competencies: the cornerstone of effective ambient intelligence in a business context. Paper presented to the UK Academy of Information Systems conference.

Business briefing available at research.ncl.ac.uk/transform/resources.php

Developing the benefits realization capability (2009–ongoing)

Action research *project* to develop competences for benefits realization. This project was funded by the Leadership Governance and Management fund of HEFCE (Chapter 11).

Ashurst, C. (2005) Transforming information systems education: equipping organisations to realise the potential of information systems. Paper presented to the UK Academy of Information Systems conference.

Ashurst, C. (2008) Building the transformation capability of the organisation. Paper presented at the British Academy of Management conference.

Ashurst, C. (2010) 'Eating our own dog food': to transform research into practice. Paper presented at the UK Academy of Information Systems conference.

Ashurst, C., Williams, S., Freer, A. and Robinson-Lamb, J. (2011) Benefits-led IT: building the organisational capability. Paper presented at the UK Academy of Information Systems conference.

Business briefing available at research.ncl.ac.uk/transform/resources.php

IT-enabled business innovation – exploring the practices required (2011 – ongoing)

Builds on the foundations reported in the book.

Appendix 2   a framework of practices for benefits realization

Code	Practice	Description	Output
BP1	Identify strategic drivers	'Top-down' activity to clarify the strategic/business drivers for the project and its contribution to the achievement of business strategy.	Strategic drivers analysis
BP2	Analyse stakeholder expectations	Conduct a structured, 'bottom-up' analysis of the stakeholders requirements, in terms of delivered benefits.	Analysis of expectations by stakeholder
BP3	Identify and define benefits	Review of strategic drivers and the stakeholder requirements, to identify/agree the target benefits.	Benefits analysis including agreed measures, targets and benefit owners
BP4	Establish benefit/process interactions	Relate the benefits to business processes to identify where changes will take place and help to identify relevant measures. Assess the variability and uncertainty in the process and consider the implications for benefits realization.	Process/benefit map
BP5	Establish benefit/stakeholder interactions	Identify stakeholder groups affected by the technology, and changes required to realize the benefits. Identify business change issues and actions required including communication and engagement with the stakeholders, and the redesign of job specifications.	Stakeholder impact assessment

Continued

Appendix 2 Continued

Code	Practice	Description	Output
BP6	Establish organization/ benefits interactions	Explore the interaction between the benefits and a full range of perspectives on the organization.	Organizational impact assessment
BP7	Establish technology/ benefits interactions	Establish a design for an IS solution that takes account of the capabilities of the technology.	Conceptual architecture overview
BP8	Plan benefits realization	Develop an overall plan to show the business case (*what* the benefits are) and *how* they are going to be realized. The plan relates to the type of project and ensures the delivery of benefits is phased as relevant and that there is appropriate consideration of organizational factors.	Benefits realization plan: defines the benefits and the actions required to realize them
BP9	Design a framework for business change governance	Design a governance framework addressing the business change project, including the enabling of IT activities. Agree on how to bring together the sponsor, benefits owners, project manager and other stakeholders through appropriate meetings, workshops and other forms of communication.	Governance framework
BP10	Benefits-driven risk assessment	Take a proactive approach to risk that focuses on business change and benefits realization.	Risk assessment and action plan

Continued

Appendix 2 Continued

Code	Practice	Description	Output
BD1	Establish an adaptive project lifecycle	Establish a project lifecycle enabling change during the project in response to learning/uncertainty – based on iterative, incremental delivery and a small number of major phases controlled by phase end milestone reviews. The adaptive lifecycle continues into benefits ramp up and evolution deployment.	Project approach – including definition of phases, deliverables and milestones
BD2	Actively lead the business change	Design, build and lead the project team and governance framework with a focus on realizing benefits. In particular, address responsibility for benefits for the organization/sponsor, benefits for the end user and the effectiveness of the team.	Role descriptions
BD3	Ensure continuing active involvement of stakeholders	Ensure there is communication and involvement with all stakeholders (based on the stakeholder analysis) to gain insight, ownership and support for changes.	Participation and communication plan
BD4	Specify changes to work and organizational design	The project focuses on the design and delivery of a business solution. This will typically require consideration of business processes, working practices, structures, roles, management framework, performance measures, and culture.	Business solution design

Continued

Appendix 2 Continued

Code	Practice	Description	Output
BD5	Make benefits-driven trade-offs	Trade-off decisions (features, cost, and schedule) are driven from a benefits perspective.	Change log/decision log
BD6	Ensure benefits-driven risk management	Take a proactive approach to risk that focuses on business change and benefits realization.	Updated risk assessment and action plan
BD7	Implement organizational changes	Implement new and revised business processes, working practices, structures, roles, management framework, and performance measures. Take action as required to encourage cultural changes.	Changed organization – this activity needs to be monitored to ensure that planned changes are actioned
BD8	Benefits-driven training and education	Ensure education and training are focused on the realization of benefits.	n/a
BR1	Establish portfolio-based evaluation criteria	Establish project evaluation criteria related to the application portfolio, that is using either different criteria for different areas of the portfolio or using a basket of measures and changing the weighting.	Evaluation framework and criteria
BR2	Benefits-driven project appraisal	Use agreed evaluation criteria to undertake a systematic assessment of benefits.	Benefits assessment report
BR3	Identify actions to realize further benefits	Where planned benefits have not been achieved, or opportunities for new benefits have been identified, a benefits' action plan needs to be established.	Benefits action plan

Continued

Appendix 2   Continued

Code	Practice	Description	Output
BR4	Facilitate lessons learned reviews	Carry out lessons learned reviews at key stages in the project and on project completion.	Lessons learned report and action plan
BR5	Complete architectural roadmap review	Carry out a review on completion of a project, to consider the contribution to the overall IT architecture. Also consider the strategic alignment of a programme and implications for future projects/releases.	Updated architecture roadmap
BE1	Ensure ownership of continued benefits exploitation	Establish a clear business role for ongoing ownership of realizing benefits.	Agreed/active benefits owner
BE2	Maintain benefits-driven training	Training is focused around benefits realization and establishing new ways of working.	Up-to-date training/education resources Ongoing training plan and provision
BE3	Evolve working practices	Continue to evolve working practices post deployment to realize further benefits.	Revised working practices

Appendix 3 summary of findings from empirical work (Chapter 6)

Competence and theme	Project-level findings	Portfolio/capability-level findings
Benefits review: measuring success	As established in previous literature, practice in most organizations is at basic level. Business cases are incomplete and there is little evidence of post-project review of benefits.	Current practice does not address the need to consider costs/benefits across a number of related projects. *Organizations have not established measures of their benefits realization capability.*
Benefits planning: taking a broader view of change	A small number of organizations have moved from IT solution delivery to benefits-driven change. The primary focus is on business process change. Two participants were designing an approach to change for each project, taking into account a range of perspectives on the organization and using a range of 'tools'.	*One organization had in place a portfolio-level role that included advising on the appropriate approach/tools for change.*
Benefits exploitation: sustaining benefits realization	Organizations had no arrangements in place for ongoing training and exploitation. *There was little emphasis on designing projects to enable ongoing exploitation.*	*The portfolio management framework has not been extended to address ongoing exploitation of information/information systems* (ITIL provides some support for this area). (ITIL – IT Infrastructure Library – widely accepted standards for service management)
Benefits planning: managing the benefits realization portfolio	n/a	Most participants were working to establish management of the project portfolio and for ensuring alignment of the investments with strategy. Organizations that had the IT portfolio under control were working to achieve a cross-organization portfolio of change initiatives.

Continued

Appendix 3   Continued

Competence and theme	Project-level findings	Portfolio/capability-level findings
Building the capacity for benefits realization	Capacity was adversely affected by weaknesses in IT service management increasing the risk of implementation; and the lack of a common framework for projects. Some organizations were focused on recruitment and development to build the pool of individuals with the skills to contribute to project success.	High Potential projects (Ward and Peppard, 2002) provide an important mechanism for increasing capacity. The lack of availability of business leaders is a major constraint. *We note that capacity for benefits realization is not well covered by previous literature.*
Skills and knowledge: building the competence of individuals	A small number of organizations were combining recruitment and education to ensure that they had a mixture of in-depth expertise and a large number of personnel with more basic knowledge of a common language and 'toolkit' for benefits realization projects.	There are signs of organizations going further and tackling this as a strategic HR issue, for example, by developing new career paths and enabling knowledge sharing.

Note: The topics discussed are those identified by the participants in the research – this is not intended to be a comprehensive list of factors contributing to the benefits realization capability.

Italics: a new theme not emphasized in previous research.

Appendix 4   outline of maturity levels for key factors (Chapter 6)

Factor	Level 1: basic	Level 2: improving	Level 3: enhanced	Level 4: advanced
Measuring success	Including all relevant costs/benefits in the business case.	Carrying out benefits realization reviews.	Focus on 'measuring the right things' as drivers of change.	Measures of the benefits realization capability.
Broader view of change	IT solution delivery.	Benefits realization from business change.	Designing the approach to change for each initiative.	Creating a more flexible approach to governance, for example enabling local innovation.
Sustaining benefits realization	Ongoing provision of education to maintain expertise through staff turnover.	Ongoing emphasis on improvement and incremental change.	Designing projects with greater emphasis on preparing for post-project learning.	New approaches for knowledge work scenarios.
Managing the benefits realization portfolio	Establishing control of the IT project portfolio.	Strategic alignment of a cross-organization portfolio of investments in change.	Adapting the approach to projects based on the portfolio.	Emphasizing business innovation and learning.
Capacity for benefits realization	Establishing a baseline of effective IT service management and a common project framework.	Focus on the skills of individuals as a driver of success.	Establishing a more agile approach to projects including incremental delivery.	Developing leaders of benefits realization.

Continued

Appendix 4   Continued

Factor	Level 1: basic	Level 2: improving	Level 3: enhanced	Level 4: advanced
Competence of individuals	Localized/ individual development of skills (e.g. PRINCE2, MSP).	Broad education programmes – with an emphasis on benefits realization.	Moving from education to a broader emphasis on development and organizational learning.	Top management engagement to address this as a strategic priority.

References

Alexander, C., Ishikawa, S. and Silverstein, M. (1977) *A Pattern Language.* New York, Oxford University Press.

Alvesson, M. and Karreman, D. (2001) Odd couple: making sense of the curious concept of knowledge management. *Journal of Management Studies,* 38, 7, pp. 995–1018.

Ambrosini, V. and Bowman, C. (2001) Tacit knowledge: some suggestions for operationalization. *Journal of Management Studies,* 38, 6, pp. 811–829.

Ambrosini, V. and Bowman, C. (2009) What are dynamic capabilities and are they a useful construct in strategic management? *International Journal of Management Reviews,* 11, 1, pp. 29–50.

Amit, R. and Schoemaker, P.J.H. (1993) Strategic assets and organizational rent. *Strategic Management Journal,* 14, pp. 33–46.

Ashurst, C., Cragg, P. and Herring, P. (2011) The role of IT competences in gaining value from e-business: an SME case study. *International Small Business Journal* (published online before print – March 2011). http://isb. sagepub.com/content/early/2011/03/10/0266242610375703.abstract (last accessed on 31 July 2011).

Ashurst, C., Doherty, N. and Peppard, J. (2008) Improving the impact of IT development projects: the benefits realisation capability model. *European Journal of Information Systems,* 17, pp. 352–370.

Augier, M. and Teece, D. (2008) Strategy as evolution with design: dynamic capabilities and the design and evolution of the business enterprise. *Organization Studies,* 29, pp. 1187–1208.

Avison, D.E. and Fitzgerald, G. (2003) *Information Systems Development: Methodologies, Techniques and Tools.* UK, McGraw-Hill Education.

Avison, D.E., Wood-Harper, A.T., Vidgen, R.T. and Wood, J.R.G. (1998) A further exploration of information systems development: the evolution of Multiview 2. *Information Technology and People,* 11, 2.

Balogun, J. and Hope Hailey, V. (2004) *Exploring Strategic Change* (2nd edition). UK, Pearson Education Limited.

Barney, J.B. (1991) Firm resources and sustained competitive advantage. *Journal of Management,* 17, pp. 99–120.

Bashein, B.J., Markus, M.L. and Riley, P. (1994) Preconditions for BPR success, and how to prevent failures. *Information Systems Management,* 11, 2, pp. 7–13.

Baskerville, R. and Myers, M. (2004) Special issue on action research in information systems: making IS research relevant to practice – forward. *MIS Quarterly,* 28, 3, pp. 329–335.

Baskerville, R. and Wood-Harper, T. (2002) A Critical Perspective on Action Research. In Myers, M. and Avison, D. (eds), *Qualitative Research in Information Systems: A Reader.* London, Sage.

BCS (2004) *The Challenges of Complex IT Projects.* British Computer Society

Benbasat, I. and Zmud R.W (1999) Empirical Research in Information Systems: The Practice of Relevance. *MIS Quarterly*, 23, 1, pp. 3–16.

Benjamin, R.I. and Levinson, E. (1993) A framework for managing IT-enabled change, *Sloan Management Review*, Summer, pp. 23–33.

Bessant, J., Phelps, B. and Adams R (2005) External Knowledge: A review of the literature addressing the role of external knowledge and expertise at key stages of business growth and development. Final Report. *Advanced Institute of Management*.

Bharadwaj, A. (2000) A resource-based perspective on information technology capability and firm performance: an empirical investigation. *MIS Quarterly*, 21, 1, pp. 169–196.

Black, J.A. and Boal, K.B. (1994) Strategic resources: traits, configurations, and paths to sustainable competitive advantage. *Strategic Management Journal*, Summer Special Issue, 15, pp. 131–148.

Blake, R. T., Massey, A. P., Bala, H., Cummings, J. and Zotos, A. (2010) Driving implementation success: insights from The Christ Hospital. *Business Horizons*, 53, pp. 131–138.

Boddy, D. and Macbeth, D. (2000) Prescriptions for managing change: a survey of their effect in projects to implement collaborative working between organisations. *International Journal of Project Management*, October 2000.

Boehm, B. and Turner, R. (2004) *Balancing Agility and Discipline: A Guide for the Perplexed*. Boston, Addison-Wesley.

Bohn, R. E. (1994) Measuring and managing technological knowledge. *MIT Sloan Management Review*, Fall, pp. 61–73.

Boland, R.J. (2002) Information use as a hermeneutic process (chapter 12). In Myers, M.D. and Avison, D. (eds), *Qualitative Research in Information Systems*. Thousand Oaks, CA, Sage.

Bontis, N., Crossman, M. and Hulland, J. (2002). Managing and organizational learning system by aligning stocks and flows. *Journal of Management Studies*, 39, 4, pp. 437–469.

Borchers, J. (2001) *A Pattern Approach to Interaction Design*. Chichester, John Wiley & Sons.

Bowman, C. and Ambrosini, V. (2000) Value creation versus value capture: towards a coherent definition of value in strategy. *British Journal of Management*, 11, pp. 1–15.

Bowman, C. and Ambrosini, V. (2003) How the resource-based and the dynamic capability views of the firm inform competitive and corporate level strategy. *British Journal of Management*, 14, pp. 289–303.

Breu, K. and Peppard, J. (2003) Useful knowledge for information systems practice: the contribution of the participatory paradigm. *Journal of information Technology*, 18, pp. 77–193.

Brooke, C. (2000) A framework for evaluating organizational choice and process redesign issues. *Journal of Information Technology*, 15, 1, pp. 17–28.

Brown, J.S. and Duguid, P. (2000) *The Social Life of Information*. Boston, Harvard Business School Press.

Brown, Tim (2008) Design thinking. *Harvard Business Review*. 86, 6, pp. 84–92.

Brynjolfsson, E. and Saunders, A. (2009) *Wired for Innovation: How Information-Technology Is Reshaping the Economy*. Cambridge, Massachusetts, MIT Press.

Burnes, B. (2005) Complexity theories and organizational change. *International Journal of Management Reviews*, 7, 2, pp. 73–90.

Caldeira, M., Cragg, P. and Ward, J. (2006) Information systems competencies in small and medium-sized enterprises. *UKAIS Conference*.

Carlile, P. (2002) A pragmatic view of knowledge and boundaries: boundary objects in new product development. *Organization Science*, 13, 4, 442–455.

Checkland, P. (1981) *Systems Thinking, Systems Practice*. Chichester, John Wiley & Sons.

Checkland, P. and Holwell, S. (1998) *Information, Systems and Information Systems*. Chichester, John Wiley & Sons.

Checkland, P. and Scholes, J. (1999) *Soft Systems Methodology in Action*. Chichester, John Wiley & Sons.

Clegg, C.W. (2000) Socio-technical principles for system design. *Applied Ergonomics*, 31, pp. 463–477.

Clegg, C.W., Axtell, C., Damodaran, L., Farbey, B., Hull, R., Lloyd-Jones, R., Nicholls, J., Sell, R. and Tomlinson, C. (1997) Information technology: a study of performance and the role of human and organisational factors. *Ergonomics*, 40, 9.

Coghlan, D. and Brannick, T. (2005) *Doing Action Research in Your Own Organization* (2nd edition). Thousand Oaks, CA, Sage.

Coplien, J.O. and Harrison, N.B. (2005). *Organisational Patterns of Agile Software Development*. Upper Saddle River, NJ, Pearson Prentice Hall.

Davenport, T. and Markus, M. (1999) Rigor v relevance revisited; response to Benbasat and Zmud. *MIS Quarterly*. 23, 1.

Davern, M. and Kauffman, R. (2000) Discovering potential and realizing value from information technology investments. *Journal of Management Information Systems*, 16, 4, pp. 121–143.

Davis, G., Lee, A., Nickles, K., Chatterjee, S., Hartung, R. and Wu, Y. (1992) Diagnosis of an information system failure: a framework and interpretive process. *Information & Management*, 23, 5, pp. 293–318.

Delbridge, R., Edwards, E., Forth, J., Miskell, P. and Payne, J. (2006) The organisation of productivity: re-thinking skills and work organisation. *AIM Research Report*.

Doherty, N. and King, M. (2001) An investigation of the factors affecting the successful treatment of organizational issues in systems development projects. *European Journal of Information Systems*, 10, pp. 147–160.

Doherty, N. and King, M. (2005) From technical to socio-technical change: tackling the human and organizational aspects of systems development projects. *European Journal of Information Systems*, 14, 1, pp. 1–5.

Doherty, N. King, M. and Al-Mushayt, O. (2003) The impact of the inadequacies in the treatment of organisational issues on information systems projects. *Information and Management*, 41, 1, pp. 49–62.

Doolin, B. (2004) Power and resistance in the implementation of a medical management information system. *Information Systems Journal*, 14, 4, pp. 343–362.

Dyer, W.G. and Wilkins A.L. (1991) Better stories, not better constructs, to generate better theory: a rejoinder to Eisenhardt. *The Academy of Management Review*, 16, 3, 613–619.

Earl, M. and Feeny, D. (1994) Is your CIO adding value? *Sloan Management Review.* Spring, 35, 3, 11–20.

Eason, K. (1988) *Information Technology and Organisational Change.* UK, Taylor & Francis.

Eden, C. and Huxham, C. (1996) Action research for management research. *British Journal of Management,* 7, 75–86.

Edwards, C. and Peppard, J. (1997) Operationalizing strategy through process. *Long Range Planning,* 30, 5, 753–767.

Eisenhardt, K. (1989) Building theories from case study research. *The Academy of Management Review,* 14, 4, pp. 532–550.

Eisenhardt, K. and Martin, J. (2000) Dynamic capabilities: what are they? *Strategic Management Journal,* 21, pp. 1105–1121.

Ewusi-Mensah, K. and Przasnyski, Z. (1994) Factors contributing to the abandonment of information systems development projects. *Journal of Information Technology,* 9, pp. 185–201.

Farbey, B., Land, F. and Targett, D. (1993) *How to Assess Your IT investment.* Oxford, Butterworth-Heinemann.

Farbey, B., Land, F. and Targett, D. (1999) Moving IS evaluation forward: learning themes and research issues. *Journal of Strategic Information Systems,* 8, 189–207.

Flyn, B.B., Wu, S.J. and Melnyk, S. (2010) Operational capabilities: hidden in plain view. *Business Horizons,* 53, pp. 247–256.

Gadamer, H.G. (1976) The Historicity of Understanding. In P. Connerton (ed.), *Critical Sociology, Selected Readings.* Harmondsworth: Penguin Books Ltd, pp. 117–133.

Garvin, D.A. (1993) Building a learning organization. *Harvard Business Review.* July–August.

Garvin, D.A. (2000) *Learning in Action: Putting the Learning Organization to Work.* Boston, Harvard Business School Press.

Gibbs, G., Knapper, C. and Piccinin, S. (2009) *Departmental Leadership of Teaching in Research-Intensive Environments.* Leadership Foundation in Higher Education (www.lfhe.ac.uk/).

Grant, R. (1996a) Prospering in dynamically competitive environments: organizational capability as knowledge integration. *Organization Science,* 7, pp. 375–387.

Grant, R. (1996b) Toward a knowledge-based theory of the firm. *Strategic Management Journal,* 17, pp. 109–122.

Gummesson, E. (2000) *Qualitative Methods in Management Research* (revised 2nd edition). Thousand Oaks, CA, Sage.

Harvey, L. and Myers, M. (2002) Scholarship and practice: the contribution of ethnographic research methods to bridging the gap (chapter 10). In Myers, M.D. and Avison, D. (eds), *Qualitative Research in Information Systems.* London: Sage.

Helfat, C. and Peteraf, M. (2003) The dynamic resource-based view: capability lifecycles. *Strategic Management Journal,* 24, 10, pp. 997–1010.

Herr, K. and Anderson, G. (2005) *The Action Research Dissertation.* California, Sage.

Highsmith, J. (2004) *Agile Project Management*. Boston, Addison-Wesley.

Huff, S., Maher, M. and Munro, M. (2006) Information technology and the board of directors: is there an IT attention deficit? *MIS Quarterly Executive*, 5, 1, pp. 55–68.

Hughes, A. and Scott Morton, M.S. (2006) The transforming power of complementary assets. *MIT Sloan Management Review*, Summer, pp. 50–58.

Iivari, J. and Huisman, M. (2007) The relationship between organisational culture and deployment of systems development methodologies. *MIS Quarterly*, 31, 1, pp. 35–88.

Jessop, A. (2004) Pattern language: a framework for learning. *European Journal of Operational Research*, 153, 2, pp. 457–465.

Johnson, G. (1992) Managing strategic change – strategy, culture and action. *Long Range Planning*, 25, 1, February, pp. 28–36.

Joshi, K. (1991) A model of users' perspective on change: the case of information systems technology implementation. *MIS Quarterly*, 15, 2, pp. 229–242.

Jurison, J. (1996) Towards more effective management of information technology benefits. *Journal of Strategic Information Systems*, 5, 4, December, pp. 263–274.

Kamoche, K., Pina e Cunha, M. and Vieira da Cunha, J. (2003) Towards a theory of organizational improvisation: looking beyond the jazz metaphor. *Journal of Management Studies*, 40, 8, pp. 2023–2051.

Kangas, K. (1999) Competency and capabilities based competition and the role of information technology: the case of trading by a Finland-based firm to Russia. *Journal of Information Technology Cases and Applications*, 1, 2, pp. 4–22.

Klein, H. and Myers, M. (1999) A set of principles for conducting and evaluating interpretive field studies in information systems. *MIS Quarterly*, Special Issue on Intensive Research, 23, 1, pp. 67–93.

Lau, F. (1999) Towards a framework for action research in information systems studies. *Information Technology & People*, 12, 2, pp. 148–175.

Lee, A.S. (1994) Electronic mail as a medium for rich communication: an empirical investigation using hermeneutic interpretation. *MIS Quarterly*, 18, 2, pp. 143–157.

Lee, A.S. (1999a) Researching MIS. In Currie, W. and Galliers, B. (eds), *Rethinking Management Information Systems*. Oxford: Oxford University Press.

Lee, A.S. (1999b) Rigor and relevance in MIS research: beyond the approach of positivism alone. *MIS Quarterly*, 23, 1, 29–33.

Leseure, M., Birdi, K., Bauer, J., Denyer, D. and Neely, A. (2004) Adoption of promising practice: a systematic review of the literature. *Advanced Institute of Management*. (www.aimresearch.org/).

Lincoln, Y. and Guba, E. (1985) *Naturalistic Inquiry*. Beverly Hills, CA, Sage.

Lockett, A. (2005) Edith Penrose's legacy to the resource-based view. *Managerial and Decision Economics*, 26, pp. 83–98.

Manns, M. and Rising, L. (2005) *Fearless change: patterns for introducing new ideas*. Boston, Addison-Wesley, Pearson Education, Inc.

Markus, M. (2004) Technochange management: using IT to drive organisational change. *Journal of Information Technology*, 19, 1, pp. 4–20.

Markus, M. and Benjamin, R. (1997) The magic bullet theory of IT-enabled transformation. *Sloan Management Review*, 38, 2, pp. 55–68.

McAulay, L. (2007) Unintended consequences of computer mediated communications. *Behaviour & Information Technology*, 26, 5, pp. 385–398.

McFarlan. F. (1981) Portfolio approach to information systems. *Harvard Business Review*, 59, 5, pp. 142–150.

McGrath, R., MacMillan, I. and Venkatraman, S. (1995) Defining and developing competence: a strategic process paradigm. *Strategic Management Journal*, 16, pp. 251–275.

Melville, N., Kraemer, K. and Gurbaxani, V. (2004) Information technology and organisational performance: an integrative model of IT business value. *MIS Quarterly*, 28, 2, pp. 283–322.

Miles, M. and Huberman, A. (1994) *Qualitative Data Analysis: An Expanded Sourcebook* (2nd edition). Thousand Oaks, California, Sage Publications Inc.

Miller, D. and Shamsie, S. (1996) The resource-based view of the firm in two environments: the Hollywood film studios from 1936–1965. *Academy of Management Journal*, 39, 3, pp. 519–543.

Mumford, E. (1995) *Effective Systems Design and Requirements Analysis: The ETHICS Approach to Computer System Design*. London, Palgrave Macmillan.

Myers, M. (1994) A disaster for everyone to see: an interpretive analysis of a failed IS project. *Accounting, Management and Information Technologies*, 4, 4, pp. 185–201.

Myers, M. (1997) Qualitative research in information systems. *MIS Quarterly*, 21, 2, pp. 241–242.

Nandhakumar, J. and Avison, D. (1999) The fiction of methodological development: a field study of information systems. *Information Technology and People*, 12, 2, pp. 176–191.

Neely A., Adams C. and Kennerley, M. (2002) *The Performance Prism: The Scorecard for Measuring and Managing Business Success*, London, FT Prentice Hall.

Neely, A., Mills, J., Platts, K., Richards, H., Gregory, M., Bourne, M. and Kennerley, M. (2000) Performance measurement system design: developing and testing a process based approach. *International Journal of Production & Operations Management*, 20, 10, pp. 1119–1146.

Newell, S. Tansley, C. and Huang, J. (2004) Social capital and knowledge integration in an ERP project team: the importance of bridging AND bonding. *British Journal of Management*, 15, pp. S43–S57.

Peppard, J. (2001) Bridging the gap between the IS organization and the rest of the business: plotting a route. *Information Systems Journal*, 11, pp. 249–270.

Peppard, J. and Ward, J. (2004) Beyond strategic information systems: towards an IS capability. *Journal of Strategic Information Systems*, 13, 167–194.

Peppard, J. and Ward J. (2005) Unlocking sustained business value from IT investments. *California Management Review*, Fall, pp. 52–69.

Peppard, J., Edwards, C. and Lambert, R. (2011) Clarifying the ambiguous role of the CIO. *MIS Quarterly Executive*, 10, 1, pp. 31–44.

Peppard, J., Ward, J. and Daniel, E. (2007) Managing the realization of business benefits from IT investments. *MIS Quarterly Executive*, 6, 1, pp. 1–11.

Pettigrew, A. (1985) *The Giant: Continuity and Change in ICI*. Oxford, Blackwell.

Pfeffer, J. and Sutton, R. (1999) Knowing 'What' to do is not enough. *California Management Review*, 42, 1, pp. 83–108.

Pfeffer, J. and Sutton, R. (2004) *The Knowing-Doing Gap: How Smart Companies Turn Knowledge into Action*. Boston, Harvard Business School Press.

Polanyi, M. (1958) *Personal Knowledge*. Chicago, University of Chicago Press.

Powell, M. and Dent-Micallef, A. (1997) Information technology as competitive advantage: The role of human, business, and technology resources. *Strategic Management Journal*, 18, 5, pp. 375–405.

Prahalad, C.K. and Hamel, G. (1990) The core competencies of the corporation. *Harvard Business Review*, 68, 3, pp. 79–91.

Kumar, R., Ajjan, H. and Niu, Y. (2008) Information technology portfolio management: literature review, framework and research issues. *Information Resources Management Journal*, 21, 3, pp. 64–87.

Rose, J. and Jones, M. (2005) The Double Dance of Agency: a socio-theoretic account of how machines and humans interact. *Systems, Signs and Actions*, 1, 1, pp. 19–37.

Rowan, J. (1981) A dialectical paradigm for research. In Reason, P. and Rowan, J. (eds), *Human Inquiry: A Sourcebook of New Paradigm Research*. Chichester: John Wiley & Sons, pp. 93–112.

Sambamurthy, V. and Bharadwaj, A. (2003) Shaping agility through digital options: Reconceptualizing the role of information technology in contemporary firms. *MIS Quarterly*, 27, 2, pp. 237–263.

Santhanam, R. and Hartono, E. (2003) Issues in Linking Information Technology Capability to Firm Performance. *MIS Quarterly*, 27, 1, 125–165,

Sauer, C. and Cuthbertson, C. (2003) *The state of IT project management in the UK 2002–2003*, Oxford, Templeton College.

Schon, D. (1983) *The Reflective Practitioner: How Professionals Think in Action*. London, Basic Books.

Schultze, U. and Boland, R. (2000) Knowledge management technology and the reproduction of knowledge work practices. *Journal of Strategic Information Systems*, 9, 2–3, pp. 193–212.

Schultze, U. and Orlikowski, W. (2004) A practice perspective on technology-mediated network relations: the use of internet-based self serve technologies. *Information Systems Research*, 15, pp. 487–523.

Sennett, R. (2009) *The Craftsman*. London, Penguin Books.

Siebers, P., Battisiti, G., Celia, H., Clegg., Fu. X., De Hoyos. R., Iona A., Petrescu, A. and Peixoto, A. (2008) Enhancing Productivity: The Role of Management Practices. *AIM Research Working Paper Series*.

Silverman, D. (2000) *Doing Qualitative Research*. London, SAGE Publications Ltd.

Srivastava, R., Fahey, L. and Christensen, H. (2001) The resource-based view and marketing: The role of market-based assets in gaining competitive advantage. *Journal of Management*, 27, 6, 777–802.

Stake, R. (1986) An evolutionary view of educational improvement. In E.R. House (ed.), *New Directions in Educational Research*. London: Falmer Press, pp. 89–102.

Taylor-Cummings, A. (1998) Bridging the user-IS gap: a study of major information systems project. *Journal of Information Technology*, 13, 1, pp. 29–54.

Taylor, C. (1976) Hermeneutics and Politics. In P. Connerton (ed.), *Critical Sociology, Selected Readings*. Harmondsworth: Penguin Books Ltd, pp. 153–193.

Teece, D. (2007) Explicating Dynamic Capabilities: The Nature and Microfoundations of (Sustainable) Enterprise Performance. *Strategic Management Journal.*

Teece, D. and Pisano, G. (1994) The dynamic capabilities of firms: an introduction. *Industrial and Corporate Change*, 3, 3, pp. 537–556.

Teece D.J., Pisano G. and Shuen A. (1990) Firm capabilities, resources and the concept of strategy. Economic Analysis and Policy Working Paper EAP 38, University of California.

Teece, D., Pisano, G. and Shuen, A. (1997) Dynamic capabilities and strategic management. *Strategic Management Journal*, 18, 7, pp. 509–533.

Thompson and Walsham (2004) Placing knowledge management in context. *Journal of Management Studies*, 41, 5, pp. 725–747.

Wade, M. and Hulland, J. (2004) The resource-based view and information systems research: review, extension, and suggestions for future research. *MIS Quarterly*, 28, 1, pp. 107–142.

Walsham, G. (1993) *Interpreting Information Systems in Organizations.* Chichester, John Wiley & Sons.

Walsham, G. (2001). *Making a World of Difference: IT in a Global Context.* Chichester, John Wiley & Sons.

Walsham, G. (2002) Interpretive case studies in IS research: nature and method (chapter 6). In Myers, M.D. and Avison, D. (eds), *Qualitative Research in Information Systems*, London, Sage.

Ward, J. and Daniel, E. (2006) *Benefits Management.* Chichester, John Wiley & Sons.

Ward, J. and Elvin, R. (1999) A new framework for managing IT-enabled business change. *Information Systems Journal*, 9, 3, pp. 197–222.

Ward, J. and Peppard, J. (2002) *Strategic Planning for Information Systems* (3rd edition). Chichester, John Wiley & Sons.

Ward, J. Taylor, P. and Bond, P. (1996) Evaluation and realisation of IS/IT benefits: an empirical study of current practice. *European Journal of Information Systems* 4, pp. 214–225.

Waterson, P.E., Clegg, C.W. and Axtell, C.M. (1997) The dynamics of work organization, knowledge and technology during software development. *International Journal of Human-Computer Studies*, 46, 1, pp. 79–101.

Weill, P. and Ross, J. (2009) *IT Savvy: What Top Executives Must Know to Go from Pain to Gain.* Boston, Harvard Business School Press.

Wenger, W. McDermott, R. and Snyder, W.M. (2002) *Cultivating Communities of Practice.* Boston, Harvard Business School Press.

Wernerfelt, B. (1984) A resourced-based view of the firm. *Strategic Management Journal*, 5, pp. 171–180.

Worren, N.A., Moore, K. and Elliott, R (2002) When theories become tools: toward a framework for pragmatic validity. *Human Relations*, 55, pp. 1227–1250.

Yin, R.K. (1994) *Case Study Research.* London, SAGE Publications Ltd.

Zahra, S., Sapienza, J. and Davidsson, P. (2006) Entrepreneurship and dynamic capabilities: a review, model and research agenda. *Journal of Management Studies*, 42, 4, pp. 917–955.

Zollo, M. and Winter, S. (2002) Deliberate learning and the evolution of dynamic capabilities. *Organization Science*, 13, 3, pp. 339–351.

Index

Action research, 149–53
Agile, 24, 50, 70–1, 72, 105,
    110–13, 175
Agile approach to research, 153–7

Benefits competences, 15–17
    Benefits delivery, 15–16, 24–6,
        36–8, 71–6, 96, 101–2
    Benefits exploitation, 16–17, 27,
        39–41, 51–2, 76–7, 98, 103
    Benefits planning, 15, 21–4, 35–6,
        49–51, 52–3, 66–71, 95, 100–1
    Benefits review, 16, 26–7, 41–2,
        77–80, 96–7, 102–3
    Organizational perspective, 105–8
    Portfolio perspective, 99–105
    Project perspective, 94–9
Benefits-driven, 8
Benefits Management, 3
Benefits realization capability, 84–5
Building competences.
    See Organizational change
Business leadership, 162–3, 175

Capability, 12
Capacity for benefits realization, 53–4
Catch-22, 82
Change. *See* Organizational change
Competence, 12, 56–8
Craft skills, 119, 175–6

Design, 175
Dynamic capabilities (implications
    for benefits realization), 165–74

Innovation, 1, 175
Interpretive research, 139–40
IS capability, 6

Knowledge management, 115–17

Learning organization. *See*
    Organizational learning

Management education, 163–4
Managerial implications, 30–1,
    160–2
Maturity, 55–6
Mindset. *See* Paradigm

Organizational change, 43–5,
    87–92, 98–9, 103–5, 120–36
Organizational learning,
    106–8, 119

Paradigm, 56–7, 88, 111–12, 114,
    139–40, 141–3, 146–7, 160,
    163–4
Participative research, 141–3
Pattern, 94, 114–18
Portfolio, 52–3, 60–81
Practice(s), 7, 13–15, 18, 65–80,
    109–12, 114–18
Principles, 10, 112–14
Project framework, 118–19

Research methods:
    Action research, 149–53
    Interpretive research, 139–40
    Participative research, 141–3
Resource based view, 11–12

Toolkit, 14, 17, 43, 65–6, 89–90,
    93–4, 104, 115, 123–4, 134–5,
    159, 161, 179

Worldview. *See* Paradigm